THE
LOSING THE TOSS

THE LUCK OF LOSING THE TOSS

My Stunt Career in the Movies and TV: including Star Wars, Indiana Jones, James Bond and The Sweeney

FRANK HENSON

BROWN DOG BOOKS

First published 2019

Published under licence by Brown Dog Books
and The Self-Publishing Partnership, 7 Green Park Station, Bath BA1 1JB

www.selfpublishingpartnership.co.uk

ISBN printed book: 978-1-78545-381-6

ISBN e-book: 978-1-78545-382-3

Cover design by Kevin Rylands

Internal design by Jenny Watson Design

Printed and bound by CPI Group (UK) Ltd, Croydon, CR0 4YY

'Frank has been a huge part of the stunt industry and lots of performers owe the respect and acknowledgement they receive these days to the sterling and professional work Frank, and others like him, have put into the business.'

– Vic Armstrong, author of *The World's Greatest Stuntman*

"Frank the Crash", or "Lead Boot", as he was also affectionately known, is a skilful and fearless stuntman. His timing is great and you can always rely on him to do a good job.'

– Paul Weston, stunt coordinator on films including *Aliens, The Living Daylights* and *Licence To Kill*

TABLE OF CONTENTS

PROLOGUE

BUTTERFLY VALLEY, THE YUMA DESERT, ARIZONA. MAY, 1982.

It's a blazing hot day in the desert – in the 90s at least. My mouth is parched. I'm sweating buckets in a bulky costume which is pinching in all the wrong places. All around, as far as the eye can see, dunes stretch to the horizon. We're standing on Jabba's skiff. Below me a sinking dune funnels down to a deep pit – the Sarlacc Pit, as it will become known throughout the world. And behind me a film crew stand tentatively by, waiting for everything to be just right. It's safe to say we're not in England anymore.

It's not only the heat that's making me sweat. I'm standing on a plank, 15 feet in the air above the boiling golden sand. Alf Joint and Colin Skeaping are standing with me. I can see the edge of red foam blocks placed down in the pit to cushion my fall. They look too thin to be of much help.

Alf mutters under his breath,

'Bloody hell, this looks dangerous.' I shrug. It's a job. It's what I'm paid to do. We have no wires, nothing to lessen the impact except for those flimsy foam cushions. But I've done jumps with the Paras – this should be a piece of cake by comparison.

A man behind me yells, 'Action!' and I think, Sod it, I'll go first. I take a running leap off the plank and launch myself, arms outstretched, into the void. The ground rushes up quicker than adrenalin. I roll over in the air. As I land my feet sink into the foam, which catches my legs, but my body falls forward, violently stretching me. My ankle snaps – it's agony. Torn ligaments. Colin jumps next and also lands badly. He's also in pain and screaming out. The crew stop filming and rush down to check on us. An ambulance is called but takes an age to arrive. Alf says to me, while we're waiting,

'If there'd been a layer of canvas over the foam, you'd have hit it and slid on.' He's right, I think as the pain sears up my leg.

Everything about this film is Top Secret – we've been told to say as little as possible about it to anyone not connected to the production. The ambulance crew are cheery but persistent. They have their suspicions.

'What are you working on?' the medic in the van asks me, as he straps me onto the gurney.

'Er, 'Blue Harvest',' I tell him. He looks at me, disbelieving.

'Come on, sir!' he says pleasantly, as I lie grimacing on the bed.

'Blue Harvest,' I insist. I wince as the ambulance goes over a bump in the road.

'Do you want these painkillers or not?' he says, smiling, dangling the packet in front of me, as the ambulance slips and slides over the sand dunes.

'Alright, alright, it's a George Lucas horror film, but don't tell anyone. Happy?' I say through gritted teeth.

'Wow. I knew that was him, the paramedic shouts to his driver.

'Just get me fixed up. I need to get back on set tomorrow.'

'I don't think so, fella. Not with that ankle.'

'I've done it before. It's not a problem,' I say breathlessly. 'Just get me sorted out and I'll worry about the rest.' He shakes his head as if I'm crazy. At least I kept my mouth shut. The identity of what will become the year's highest, and the decade's second-highest, grossing film remains a secret – for now. At the hospital one of the medics jokes,

'We're not operating on you until you tell us the name of the film.' It's a light-hearted comment, but it shows the level of interest that exists in this film – it's like nothing I've ever known.

I'm laid up for ten days this time, which drives me mad with boredom. I was itching to get back to the action but the swelling won't go down and no one wants to risk a further injury. Colin hadn't broken his leg. That honour fell to my stunt pal Paul Weston, later the same day. He was fighting with an American stunt performer on a wire, about fifteen feet up, when the wire snapped and they fell to the ground – most of their weight landed on Paul's leg. That's three of us injured on the first day of shooting.

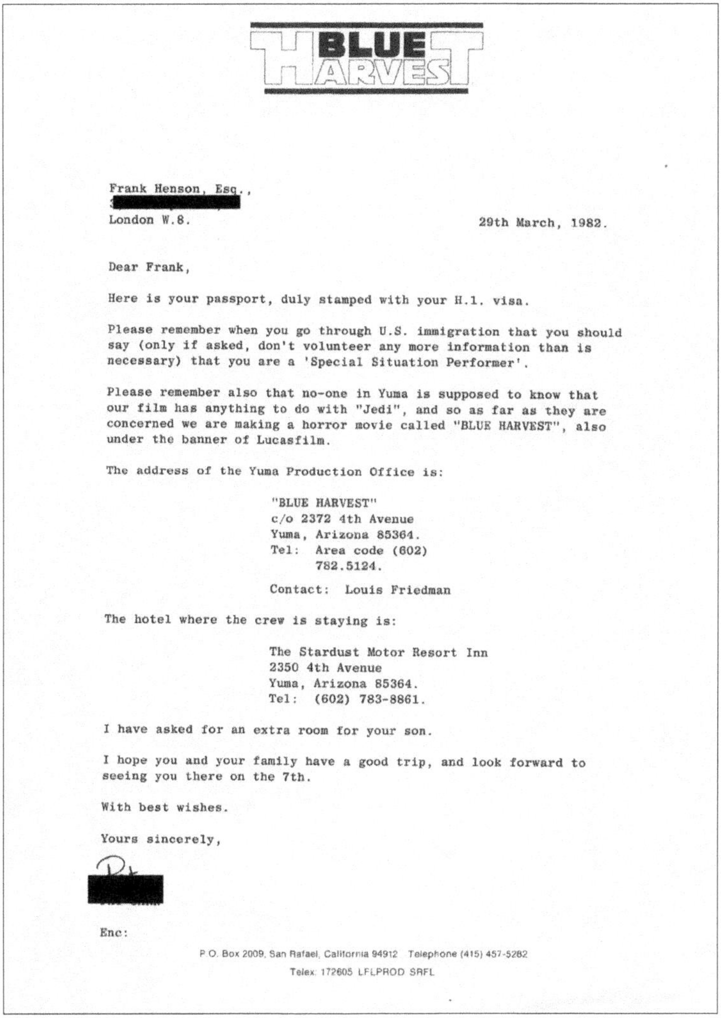

BLUE HARVEST

Frank Henson, Esq.,
[redacted]
London W.8.

29th March, 1982.

Dear Frank,

Here is your passport, duly stamped with your H.1. visa.

Please remember when you go through U.S. immigration that you should say (only if asked, don't volunteer any more information than is necessary) that you are a 'Special Situation Performer'.

Please remember also that no-one in Yuma is supposed to know that our film has anything to do with "Jedi", and so as far as they are concerned we are making a horror movie called "BLUE HARVEST", also under the banner of Lucasfilm.

The address of the Yuma Production Office is:

"BLUE HARVEST"
c/o 2372 4th Avenue
Yuma, Arizona 85364.
Tel: Area code (602)
782.5124.

Contact: Louis Friedman

The hotel where the crew is staying is:

The Stardust Motor Resort Inn
2350 4th Avenue
Yuma, Arizona 85364.
Tel: (602) 783-8861.

I have asked for an extra room for your son.

I hope you and your family have a good trip, and look forward to seeing you there on the 7th.

With best wishes.

Yours sincerely,

[redacted]

Enc:

P.O. Box 2009, San Rafael, California 94912 Telephone (415) 457-5282
Telex: 172605 LFLPROD SRFL

Letter from 'Blue Harvest' production team

Welcome to my world – the world of stunts. Agony and injury are part-and-parcel of the job. It's why we're there. Not to get hurt, but to make sure none of the other actors do. And to make them look good, of course. I've suffered more than my fair share of accidents and incidents over the year – that's why they call me 'Frank the Crash'. Well, that's part of the reason. The other part is that I'm a bloody good driver with no fear – that's why I'm also known as 'Lead Boot Henson' – when I put my foot down it stays down. But I'm getting ahead of myself…

A MESSAGE FROM FRANK

I'm getting on a bit now – 83 and counting. I've had a great life and I've met and worked with some wonderful people, as you'll read in this book. I've also worked with some scoundrels. More of that anon.

I've done alright for myself – better than someone from my background, with my start in life, could reasonably expect to do. It may surprise you that I've made most of my money outside of the film business. Yes, I've had another very successful career as a property developer. This has given me the means to live very comfortably – in a Kensington mews house, then a large house in the prestigious St Peter's Square, in Hammersmith, and now in a lovely house in Sussex, which I built from scratch. I have a wonderful wife and I have a wonderful family – my son Franklin and my lovely grandchildren. Yes, life has been good to me, but I've made it that way.

If I could pass on one message to my grandchildren, to your grandchildren or to anyone else who's reading this, it would be that anyone can succeed who has the determination to do so. You don't have to be a clever clogs, have a pile of exam certificates, or rely on the bank of Mum and Dad. All you need is the right attitude, perseverance and enough brains to surround yourself with good, encouraging people: you'll do alright. Better than alright.

I know that life isn't easy, believe me. But as long as you can get up in the morning with a strong heart and a healthy appetite for work, you can really get on. It doesn't matter what you do – whether you're working as a plumber to pay the mortgage on your new house, or working as a binman to cover the rent while you figure it all out.

In my eyes, any work is good work. I took a number of jobs before I became a stuntman, or before I even thought about entering the movie business. I learned to cut hair in the 1960s and became a hairdresser in Butlin's in Yorkshire, and then down in London. I wasn't good at it, but it gave me a living. Then I washed dishes in a Soho café for months to keep myself going and worked the doors on Soho nightclubs. At the age of 22 I was digging out trenches in Shoreham, in all weathers. This is about as far away from Hollywood, or even Pinewood, as you can get. All the time I was learning – about other people and about myself. My appetite to get on was unquenchable, and it drove me forwards.

I know young people are growing up in a new era – with new technology which is, frankly, beyond me now. It's a completely different world from the one I grew up in. No doubt everything will be different again, in fifty years' time.

Things change, but the one thing that doesn't, the one thing that unites Frank Henson with John Wayne, Robert Mitchum, Carrie Fisher, Harrison Ford and everyone I ever worked with in TV and films, is that if you want to get anywhere in life, you have to work hard. And honestly, it really is much more rewarding to get out there and do any work you can find, because once you get that paycheck at the end of the week, or the month, it feels fantastic, and that money is yours to do what you will with. Believe me, if you've done it, I've probably done it, and there's no shame in whatever keeps you out of trouble and puts a bit of food on the table!

That said, I have been fortunate at key points in my career. Losing the toss on one job gave me my most famous role – as 'biker scout' in *Return of the Jedi*. I also got into stunt driving at just the right time. Luck, accident or design? You decide. One thing's for sure, without determination and hard work, I wouldn't have been in the right place at the right time in the first place. Lecture over.

I'm so proud of my son, Franklin, who has followed me into a stunt career but has far exceeded anything I did. He's a successful, in-demand stunt coordinator now, and we still work together from time to time. He's helped me out in this book – where I couldn't remember much about films we worked on he's filled in some blanks.

I've written about the films that meant a lot to me in my career – the ones that were memorable for one reason or another. Sometimes it's a particular stunt, or the work of a colleague that sticks in the mind. Other times, it's what was going on in my life while I was doing a particular job. That's what life's really like, though, isn't it? A mix of business, pleasure, grief, obstacles and achievements. At the end of the day what really matters, though, is family, friends and work. That's what life is all about in my opinion. I hope you enjoy reading these memories as much as I've enjoyed putting them together.

With My Family (L-R):

Marion, the author, Callum, Ryan, Fionn, Aine, Franklin and Saoirse

I'D LIKE TO THANK...

I have a lot of people to be thankful to. I have a list of about thirty-five names in my head. Sadly, a lot of them aren't around anymore so I keep them alive by saying their names and imagine talking to them while I'm lying in bed at night. Just because they've passed on doesn't mean I will ever forget them – this is my way of ensuring that I don't.

The first people on my list are my grandparents who took me in at a difficult time and did their best to set me on the right path. Next on my list is a man named Fred Savage, who didn't know me from Adam and yet showed me such kindness. He was so good to me growing up, I'll never forget him. My mother had got a job at his pub – The Whitehawk Inn in Brighton. One day he saw me dressed in rags – ill-fitting, worn, dirty clothes and shoes with holes in them – and he took pity on me. He gave me my first job collecting beer bottles. I'd get tuppence back on each one of them. Then for Christmas he'd get me a top, or some shoes, and so on. You see, I came from a very poor background and my family didn't have very much at all, next to nothing in fact, and it was so kind of him to help me at such a tender age. He even taught me the value of self-respect. Once I got into trouble for shoplifting – I was such a little toe-rag back then – and he went to juvenile court with me and spoke up on my behalf. He really was like the father I didn't have.

I also have to be thankful to all of the directors, actors but mainly the stunt performers that I've worked with over my fifty-years-and-counting career in stunts. People like Peter Brayham

Grandparents Frank and Edith Smith, with Auntie Lil

who not only employed me on many TV programmes and movies, but also became a dear friend and the godfather to my son, Franklin. We miss Peter so much. Peter Diamond who got me involved with the *Star Wars* franchise. The small parts I played in *Return of the Jedi* still bring me fan mail every week from all over the world. Vic Armstrong who hired me often and saved my skin on *Indiana Jones and the Temple of Doom*. Carol Wilks who was a delightful director to work with on British TV programmes and who is a great friend. Joe Powell and too many other people to mention here, but hopefully I've done them justice in the pages of this book. Also, Stevie Dent who gave my son Franklin his big chance as a stunt director. Franklin took it and is now working non-stop on one big movie after another. It's been a pleasure to work with everyone who I have come across in a 50-year career that I have enjoyed so much.

OPENING SCENE

I was born at home in Whitehawk, Brighton, on 2 May 1935. Whitehawk was the estate created by the Brighton Corporation to house people displaced by slum clearances in the city. A lot of rag-and-bone men were moved there, for instance. It was an area which became very well known for working-class poverty, and a lot of families moved back into Brighton, as soon as they could afford to.

They were difficult times and we were a poor family with very little. My mother wrapped me in blankets and put me in a chest of drawers to sleep in. She would swap clothing coupons – everything was on ration – for people's second-hand clothes. That way she got more items for the family. Sadly, my father never stayed around and I never met him. All I have from him is his surname 'Henson' – that's all. My mother did marry another man and, like many poor families at that time, they had a lot more kids: five boys and a girl. They were my five stepbrothers Jimmy, Patrick, Michael, Terry and Sean, and my stepsister Margaret.

My family was Catholic and I was brought up that way, and attended a Catholic school. A lot of that stays with you whether you believe in the afterlife or you don't – and I don't. Not really, but I do have a fascination with religion, and will happily bend the ear of anyone who has a similar interest.

Tragedy struck us early when my stepbrother Jimmy, at the age of six, went to play with some friends in a posher part of Brighton. They were fooling around on top of these huge water tanks – which had been built during the war to provide emergency water supplies in case of fire. Somehow he slipped in without it being noticed. It was two days before his body was recovered. Even though there was nothing I could have done to prevent it happening, I felt guilty. The terrible thing is, I never really got on with him, and we used to argue, as you do with your siblings. I think it was, deep down, because I was jealous that he had a proper father and I didn't. His death has haunted me ever since. I wish I could have been a better stepbrother to him. Patrick and Michael have also since died. I lost contact with Sean and Terry. Margaret and I exchange cards at Christmas.

My stepfather and I never really clicked from day one. He never really showed me any love or compassion. He used to cook these legs of pork and I would get the fat – I couldn't stand it. Pork knuckle. I remember that far more vividly than the kickings and the beatings. I think it's part of the reason it was so easy for me to become a vegetarian later in life.

One day he hit me really hard, almost knocking me to the ground. My grandad stepped in and had a hell of a fight with him – for a seventy-year-old man he could really move. I'd like to say that was the end of that, but things didn't really improve between us, and I would sneak off to my grandparents whenever I could. They'd give me jam sandwiches which in those days were considered a bit of a luxury.

I should say here that I've never like the idea of fighting, but it's also fair to say I got in my fair share of scrapes growing up and beyond. Sometimes my temper would just get the better of me. And sometimes, when someone's stabbing you in the back or trying it on, you do just have to stand your own ground. It takes two to tango after all. But fighting's not something I'd recommend young people get into the habit of doing – little good ever comes of it. Believe me.

My grandparents didn't have much time for my stepdad following that incident. I was getting into trouble and, at the age of 13, I was sent to a remand centre for a spell. They were tough institutions back then. Fred Savage, who I mentioned earlier, spoke up for me at the court, telling them about my stepfather and how he had treated me. As a result of Fred's testimony, the court gave me permission to live with my grandparents. Otherwise I'd have been sent to an approved school for young offenders, and that rarely ends well. Their home was my home until their deaths when I was 20. I have so much to thank them for.

I was much happier at my grandparents. They'd had a beautiful mongrel dog called Bob when I was younger. He was the first creature I felt loved by and could show affection to. Bob gave me my love of all animals which has continued to this day. There was also an old lady who lived nearby who couldn't get out much, so my grandad would take her dog out with us at weekends. There was something between me and dogs which just clicked. I don't want to sound soppy – no one who knows me would call me that – but I think it's the unconditional love you get from an animal that you bond with. There's a simple, uncomplicated trust which you can rely on. To be honest, I hadn't had a lot of that in my life to this point. I've certainly kept dogs ever since – right now, I've got little Paddy who's a rescue terrier. Sometimes I think we've got a lot in common!

After my grandparents passed away I went to live with the Burgess family. They had four daughters – Gwen, Margie, Betty and Rosemary. My Uncle Frank was married to Margie and he came to me and said,

'Mrs Burgess is quite happy to take you in.' I lived with them for two years until I went to try and make my fortune in London. Again, I had good reason to be grateful for the kindness of people who didn't know me that well. I'm still in touch with the family.

It was a pretty grim childhood in many ways, but it paid off in others. I learned to look after myself from an early age. I left school at 15, as you could in those days. In truth, I couldn't wait to get out. I wasn't academic and so I felt I was just wasting my time. One of my first jobs was collecting all the lost golf balls on the local course and selling them back to the club. I didn't get much but it still felt good that it was my money – earned by me. I used this money to buy a pedal bike. My mum took me to the bike shop and I paid for it in weekly instalments. My grandad would cover this bike in Vaseline and store it in the spare bedroom whenever I was away –

The wonderful Burgess family, with Marion and my uncle Frank

they were more prone to rust back then. My grandad was a keen golfer who worked at the local club as a caddy. At the age of 15 I became a caddy, too. I played a bit but I wasn't very good.

Another early job I had was selling firewood. Many houses and other buildings were blown up during the war, and so there was a lot of firewood lying around for a young enterprising lad like me to collect. I used to take it around to rich people's houses and sell it to them.

It was while doing this that I had what might be considered my first show business encounter – though only by a very long, thin thread. One of my wood-burning clients was a lovely old gentleman who we knew as Captain Ventham. He was always smartly dressed and well shaved. Later, he had a daughter called Wanda Ventham who became an actress. Her best-known role was probably as Cassandra Trotter's mum, Pamela Parry, in the BBC sitcom *Only Fools and Horses*. She married Timothy Carlton and had a son named Benedict Cumberbatch who is famous, of course, for playing Sherlock Holmes as well as many other film and TV roles. I would love to have a talk with him about his grandad.

The poverty of my childhood gave me an appreciation for having money which I've never lost. I love my grandchildren and I'm delighted that they've never had to experience that kind of hunger or lack, but I think they've missed out in some ways, too. It certainly toughens you up and gives you a determination to better yourself in whatever way you can. One of my proudest moments was when I, this kid brought up on a rough estate in Brighton, managed to send his son to the same prep school as Prince Charles, and then to Millfield – one of the top boarding schools in the country. More of that later.

IIIIIIIIIIII

My Uncle Frank Smith – my mother's brother – was another hero in the family. Sure, he gave me a couple of hidings but I probably deserved them. I remember him chasing me down the road on one occasion shouting,

'You ate my butter and you ate my bacon!' Everything was on ration so you could understand why he was so upset. But he had a really good heart. He gave me a job working for him as a plumber's mate which I managed to last about eighteen months at. After that he helped me get a job working as a fireman on the railways. My mate Don Newland was already working there and it appealed to me for some reason. Don had given me some of the questions that were likely to come up at my interview. One of them was this: *If it takes a minute to count to fifty, how long would it take to count to a million?*

See if you can work it out – quickly, though.* Frank stood beside me, working out the answer on the garage wall with a pencil. I memorised the answer and managed to come out with it at the interview. They must have been impressed because I got the job and stayed there until I started my National Service.

Uncle Frank had served in North Africa during the Second World War. He was in the famous Black Watch regiment. He was awarded a Military Medal, which was awarded for bravery on land. Rumour was that he had taken out a tank with a bazooka but, like many people who had fought in that war, and seen things they wish they hadn't, he didn't like to talk about it.

(*The answer's 13 days, 21 hours and 30 minutes. Did you get it?)

JOINING THE ARMY

I joined the Army in 1953, when I was eighteen years old. Like everybody else, I had to do my two years' National Service. I badly wanted to be a paratrooper, partly because my cousin Frank Smith – Uncle Frank's boy – was already one. We were close as kids, even though he'd had a different background to me, having been brought up in Scotland. Cousin Frank was intelligent. He ended up in the police force as an inspector. I was planning to follow him at one stage until he came back from Hendon Training College with the police training manual, which was several inches thick. I asked him,

'Frank, is it difficult to learn?' and he said,

'It is a bit.'

'Well, if it's difficult for you, it'll be impossible for me,' I said. He went on to become an inspector, as did his son.

With cousin Frank Smith, 1956

Anyway, it was very difficult to get transferred to the Paras but eventually, after bugging my superiors, I was allowed to take the test and, once I had finished my basic training at Aldershot, I was stationed with the 16th Independent Parachute Brigade in Egypt for nine months.

Unfortunately, I managed to get into trouble, even in the Army. I was caught fighting a couple of times. In those days I never backed down from a challenge. I think it stems from my upbringing – there were a few men in my early life who didn't mind swinging a punch. I'm not proud of it. I've still got a temper but I've been able to turn away from trouble for a long time now.

If there's one man I would like to meet again it would be my Sergeant Major, Jack Dibden. He really had the measure of me. He could be good cop or bad cop, depending on what he thought I needed at a particular time. Once, after a scrap, he came to the cells where I'd been locked up.

'Henson, get down and give me press-ups!' he ordered. He stood there waving his cane just above my back to make sure I did them properly and didn't stop for a break. By press-up number 60 I was exhausted.

'Don't look so tough now, do you, Henson?' he said, and turned on his heel and marched out, leaving me collapsed on the floor in a sweaty heap.

On another occasion we were marching in the desert. It was unrelentingly hot and I was carrying the Bren gun – over 20 pounds of hard metal which was scorching under the sun. I was close to collapsing again, this time because of the sweltering desert heat. Jack Dibden appeared again and said,

'Come on, Henson, let me give you a break from that,' and took the gun off me. I'd like to think he liked me, saw I was alright under all the bluster, though of course he was clever enough never to let me know for sure.

Sadly, I wasn't confident enough to ask for his phone number

– I would have loved to have taken him out for a drink. I had so much respect for the man. But that's what happens in life: you meet people who have an impact on you and never hear from them again.

IIIIIIIIIIII

Getting into trouble with vehicles started for me around this time, too. During my basic training I was sent up to London in a team of trucks because there was a petrol strike on and they needed tanker drivers to be ferried to the petrol depots. The lorry I was driving had no backlights, so the officer in charge said to me, 'Make sure you stay away from the back of the convoy.' Unfortunately I was last coming out of the barracks, so I tried to get in front of the next lorry but had to break sharply – with no warning lights. A taxi driver following behind me went straight into my rear and buckled up. That was my first charge.

Then, soon after I arrived in the desert, I was given the task of driving a lorry to headquarters. I blithely followed another, narrower vehicle through the entrance, under a drop gate. There was a terrible bang. I'd taken the gate completely off its hinges. They were left twisted on what remained of the gateposts.

The corporal sat next to me in the lorry said,

'I'm not going to explain this. You'll have to go and tell the old man.' *Thanks a lot mate*, I thought.

So I had to go and report the incident to sergeant major Dibden.

'Yes, Henson, what is it?' he asked. I'm standing there looking very sheepish – it being my first week there and all that.

'I've hit the gate, sir,' I replied.

'Bent it much, did you?' he asked. I gulped very hard.

'Took it right off, sir.'

In a rage, he threw his hat to the floor and jumped up and down on it. A while later, after he had calmed down slightly, he told me to report to Captain Ackerman.

'Henson, it appears to be the case that you are not a very good driver,' says the captain.

'It's all I can do, sir,' I replied firmly. Evidently, he thought otherwise.

'Henson, would you like to be a batman?'

'No thank you, sir. I want to be a driver, sir.'

'Yes, but you're a fucking terrible driver, aren't you?' He sighed. 'Would you like to be a barman in the officers' mess?'

'Sir, with respect, sir, I want to be a driver,' I said, looking straight ahead.

'Take the barman's position in the mess. At least you'll be out of harm's way.' I was gutted. I'd lost a great job, as I saw it, driving lorries in the desert and now I was going to be stuck in the officers' mess. But my pal said,

'No, it's the best job in camp! You've got access to all the booze and you find out exactly what's going on.'

It turns out he was right. It was a good job, it even got me into general bar work and stocktaking. There were some real characters and though I don't remember that much about it there was one incident which summed up what the Army was like, as far as I was concerned. I was in the mess, serving one of the officers with wine. The chap sitting next to him leaned back and knocked the bottle with his shoulder, which got covered in red wine. There was a silence for a moment, then the major laughed, and then everyone laughed, taking their cue from him. It was so false and I couldn't wait to get out.

Towards the end of my stint I got into a fight with a Scottish sergeant and I was put on charges – about ten of them – which was pretty serious.

The colonel at the camp looked me up and down and said,

'Henson, you're a silly man. You've only got 22 days of National Service left and you've got in a lot of trouble.' Then he turned to Sergeant Major Jack Dibden. 'Ten days confined to barracks. March him out.' And with that, he dismissed me and went back to studying the paperwork on his desk. Dibden whispered to me on the way to barracks,

'Well, we won't be asking you to sign on, will we?' He was a lovely man and I respected him.

Apart from some of the people I met, my life in the Army meant nothing to me. To be honest, I was desperate to get in but after the first week, I couldn't wait to get out.

My problems stemmed from confidence – a lack of it. I never knew when to back down from a challenge, or not to rise to a perceived slight. I was on edge and reacted badly to any provocation. I can see that, now I've got plenty of confidence, but it's different when you're young and inexperienced in life. If you're someone like me, from my background, you learn these lessons the hard way.

EX-PARA

So once I'd finished my two years National Service, in 1955, I left as soon as I could. I was proud of having been a Para, but I couldn't stand being ordered about. An ex-SAS soldier, who was impressed by the red beret, got me a job working at Shoreham Harbour for £12 a week, rising to £18 with night work at weekends – not bad money at all back then. We shared living accommodation to save on expenses.

I was working twelve hours a day, six days a week – 72 hours. It was hard work digging trenches but I loved it. I was fitter then than I had ever been in the Army.

My last Army-related mishap occurred on the barge. It was a really cold winter that year and very slippery underfoot. One morning I was jumping off the barge to open a lock gate and I slipped into the water. It was freezing and I got out quickly but, in the scramble, my red beret – which I'd been wearing because of the cold – came off and floated away. I couldn't believe it. I'd gone through so much in the Paras for my beret and now I'd gone and lost it like that. Well, thankfully it did turn up a bit later, but not before I'd had a chuckle thinking about people walking along the towpath who might have seen it floating and think a paratrooper must have landed in the canal! No, me and the military were best shot of each other.

LEADING LADY

1955 was a turning point for another reason. This was the year I met Marion – the love of my life. I was still working as a labourer. One evening I was driving around with some friends and we pulled into a caravan park and got chatting to some people staying there. One of my mates had got out of the car to talk to someone and I turned around to see this beautiful young lady had taken his place. I was smitten that first time I saw Marion. We had a great night out – I had £61 on me, I remember, and she helped me spend the lot. She said that evening made it the best holiday she'd ever had.

Coming from my background, from a broken home, it took me a long time to cement our relationship. I really wanted it to work but I found it difficult to trust anyone. Marion couldn't understand this. She came from a very loving family and she knew right away that we would last forever. The best thing I ever did was to ask Marion to marry me and we finally tied the knot in 1962.

Marion, the love of my life, on our wedding day, 1962

CUT!

It's funny how things work out. I had got friendly with a guy called Dave Thatcher who I'd met in a snooker hall. He was an ex-boxer. We moved to London together. Dave had been a professional between 1953 and 1954 and took part in four bouts. He was highly thought of at the time, but sadly it didn't work out for him in the end. As with all 'gentleman' boxers, before sponsorship became such a huge part of all sports, he needed another job to keep him going.

Dave told me he'd decided to learn hairdressing. Hairdressing was becoming big business and I said to Dave,

'I fancy a bit of that.' So he encouraged me to join him on a training course. I know it sounds strange – an ex-boxer and a navvy training to become hairdressers – but it was seen as quite a prestigious profession for men to get into.

During the day we were at hairdressing school but at night, Dave worked in a club in Wardour Street while I worked just down the road, as a dishwasher at the Act One Scene One coffee bar, where many well-known actors would hang out. It was close to the equally fashionable 2i's coffee bar. Many famous British singers of that time, like Tommy Steele and Cliff Richard, were discovered playing at the 2i's.

I used to stand over a sink from 5pm to midnight. From the sweaty little kitchen, I could see up into Wardour Street through the grate where the girls of Soho were conducting their night-time business. After a while I was promoted to the coffee machine and salad bar. Not bad, eh?

As well as the Act One being a hang-out for the cool kids and actors, something quite different sticks in my mind from my time there. Late one night a couple of men came in and ordered the Spaghetti Bolognese. The waiter told them it was finished but the customers insisted, so the chef picked leftover spaghetti from the bin, washed it and served it up to them. I was horrified. I had thought of this chef as an educated person, and I was firmly from the backstreets, but there was no way I'd have behaved like that.

Apart from that incident, I couldn't complain – there were certainly benefits which came with the job. The best perk was that I didn't have to buy any food because I got a free dinner every night. I was vegetarian even then, but when Marion came up to London to stay for the weekend, I was able to take her home a bit of smoked salmon, which was considered a real treat. The other benefit of working there was that I learned how to eat spaghetti properly – and certainly not out of the bin.

IIIIIIIIIIII

I finished my hairdressing course and the upshot of it was that I wasn't very good. I could cut hair, but as for the styling… let's just say that it wasn't my strong point. But it was work. I found a job at Butlin's in Filey, Yorkshire, through the Hairdressers' Journal, so I moved up North. Here I was lucky to fall in with Peter Landsman who was a top hairdresser and a very shrewd bloke. I was there for about six months. I wasn't the fastest hair cutter, but because the clientele was different every week, I quickly got used to talking to all sorts of customers and cutting different hair types. This helped me a bit, but it was clear to me that I was never going to be a top stylist. Peter got me extra work clearing the glasses and plates in the restaurant at night, which to be honest, I enjoyed as much as the hairdressing, if not more. It was all work bringing a wage at the end of the week. That's all that mattered to me.

Eventually I moved back to London. Peter Landsman phoned me up one day and invited me to a dance in West London. There were lots of boxers there including a chap called Bruce Wells, who

I'd met before when he came to Filey Butlin's with a team of boxers to give physical training demonstrations. He was looking for a room in London and I told him I had a spare one.

Me and Bruce got on very well for a while and he ended up working as a stunt artist on various films and TV productions. He also changed the course of my life, by introducing me to Jim Houlihan. Jim was a tough Irishman who Bruce had trained to become a boxer. Jim had had six professional fights and didn't win one of them. Boxing, like hairdressing for me, was never going to be the career for him.

WORKING ON THE DOORS

Jim Houlihan quickly became a great mate of mine. He knew everyone who worked on the doors in the clubs and pubs around Soho, and so I ended up working as a doorman with Jim between 1961 and 1965, which I enjoyed very much.

As a doorman you wanted a quiet life. Some nights went peacefully but on other occasions it would all go off. You'd get people who couldn't handle their drink and who just wanted to cause trouble. There would be fights but I'd try and keep the disturbance to a minimum – apart from anything else the fights were bad for business. My job was to intervene before trouble started, but sometimes they would turn against you, so you would give them a slap and send them on their way. I learned from Jim that if you could spot the troublemakers on the way in, you could keep it outside.

As anyone who has ever worked on the doors of a club or a pub will tell you, doormen are regarded in two different ways by the public. Sensible people realise that doormen are there to prevent any incidents developing which may prevent them from having a good time. Less reasonable people think the security is there to cause as much aggravation as possible, because they are just thugs. Whichever way you look at it I can put the record straight – well, at least from my experience. I was there to make sure everyone got along. Yes, I had to deal with some odd situations, and some of the people I met I couldn't have invented, but I was there as a deterrent, not to incite violence.

Most punters were fine, of course, but there were types who you could see were going to cause problems, especially when the booze started to flow. A classic case was the boyfriend who wasn't getting the attention he believed he deserved from his girlfriend, so he picked a fight with one of the doormen.

Sometimes it would get way out of hand and you had to do whatever was necessary to bring things to a quick conclusion – the minimum of disturbance was what you were after. For example, one night this bloke would not quit. He was causing havoc, knocking over tables and chairs. Anyway, I got involved to calm things down, and in order to restore a bit of order I gave him a right hook. He hit the deck and pretended he was dead. The police were called and told by his mates that I'd hit this fella without due cause. I spent a couple of hours in West End Central but I was released after the fella had sobered up and realised he would be an idiot to press charges. I might have even bought him a drink if he'd turned up at the club that night, but predictably I never saw him again.

GETTING INTO PROPERTY

Jim Houlihan helped me out in another major way. He lent me the money I needed to buy the first property I ever owned. Apart from stunt work, my other main interest has been property development. I've always loved to buy run-down properties, do them up and sell them again at a profit.

I wanted to buy a three-bedroomed place in Dagenham, next door to Marion's parents. My entire savings at that point amounted to £100. The building society told me I'd need a deposit of £250 to buy the house, which doesn't sound like much now, but it was a reasonable amount of money back then. Jim loaned me the extra £150. The arrangement was that I'd pay him back £10 a week, from my wages working the doors, which he'd also arranged of course. Eventually I sold the house to my brother-in-law for a healthy £1000 profit.

I paid Jim back and carried on saving. Marion and I moved into rooms in North Kensington. A couple of years later, I met a young man who was desperate to sell this beautiful, derelict mews house in Kensington, just off the High Street. It was a risk – there was dry rot and woodworm everywhere, no floorboards and only one toilet. Basically a total renovation was required, and this lad wanted £7000 for it which seemed a fortune. I'd managed to save £4000 by this point but still, the other £3000 was going to be difficult to find.

The lad was so desperate to sell that he lent me £3000 to buy the house off him. Marion fell in love with this house the first time she saw it, and no wonder. I set about renovating it. I can't knock two pieces of wood together, but I knew a lovely man – Charlie – who was a brilliant renovator and carpenter.

I set about visiting demolition sites and reclamation yards across London to buy old timber which I would clean up and use for the house – it was like the times I used to collect firewood to sell, except this time I was looking for better-quality stuff. It's amazing how your experiences come unexpectedly in useful. The front of the house was all mahogany – even the garage doors were mahogany. It looked stunning. The struggles of my early days had made me determined never to be poor again.

Our Kensington mews house

We ended up living in this property for several years. Marion could write a book about that place – she knew every nook and cranny. She had a great friend who lived a couple of doors down, and Kensington High Street was a five-minute walk. Eventually we sold it for a handsome profit. Right from the word go I had a good instinct for property development – which houses to buy and which ones to pass on. The mews house was the first of many such properties I would buy, do up and sell. When we sold a property in St Peter's Square in West London for £2.5 million, I put the profits into a trust fund for my grandchildren which I add to from time to time. And property development enabled me to buy the beautiful house we live in today, here in Sussex, and the farm I bought to entertain the grandchildren, which I still work on every morning.

Our house in St Peter's Square, Hammersmith, London. Drawing by BUD

GETTING INTO FILM

The reason you're most likely to be reading this book is because of my life in films. And again, I have Jim Houlihan to thank for setting me on that path, though when I look back at what I'd done to this point – the hard, physical work, the stint in the Paras, working on the doors in Soho – it could almost have been a training course for being a stuntman. But I'm getting ahead of myself again. Let's head back to 1961, when Jim – not content with working the Soho doors – decided to become a film extra. And not content with helping me on the road to property development, he was literally about to change my life one final time.

I wish I could remember the conversation I had with Jim about his new job as a film extra that made me say, 'I wouldn't mind doing that – it sounds great.' Anyway, he had a word with Sean Brannigan, the burly Irish secretary of the Film Artistes' Association (FAA). The FAA pretty much controlled who worked as an extra and who didn't in those days, and Sean had a lot of clout in the business because of the strength of the unions. Unfortunately, Sean had told Jim they didn't have any space on their roster at that time, but Jim winked at me and said,

'Don't worry, Frank, I'll get you in.'

I was quite nervous for some reason when we entered Sean's office – maybe I had an inkling of what was ahead of me, most likely not. But when Sean, an ex-rugby player, rose from behind his desk to his full 6'2" to greet us, I took an immediate liking to him. Jim and Sean were chatting about an upcoming wrestling bout which was sold out. Both him and Sean, it turned out, were big wrestling fans, and tickets for the most popular fights were like gold dust. Jim then introduced me as the friend of his who wanted to get into film work. Sean acknowledged me, but then sighed and said,

'Sorry pal, we really are full at the moment.' With a flourish Jim then produced a couple of tickets for the bout and placed them on the desk. Sean looked down, then slowly up at me. 'Well, there might be one more space now. Let me just check.' He turned around to a filing cabinet and produced an FAA registration form, which he handed to me with a smile. I signed on the dotted line and became a film extra there and then. I have never looked back.

Incidentally I became great friends with Sean and we spent a lot of time together over the years, including more than one very merry Christmas. He was a lovely man who had many stories to tell about his work with people like Michael Winner and The Beatles, most of which I'm afraid I can't repeat!

EXTRA, EXTRA

The very first film I worked on as an extra was *The Guns of Navarone* (1961) – a war film directed by the great J. Lee Thompson, who I was to work for on two other films in the 1980s – *The Ambassador* (1984) and *King Solomon's Mines* (1985).

The Guns of Navarone had an all-star cast including Gregory Peck, David Niven and Anthony Quinn. Not a bad one to start with, eh? I'd like to say it was a great baptism into the film world but things went a bit wrong on day one of shooting. I was playing a radio operator in uniform. I was given a pair of boots which were way too small for me and hurt like hell. I said to one of the wardrobe ladies,

'No wonder the Germans had that funny march. It must have been their boots.'

When I asked for a pair that I could actually get into, it didn't go down at all well. You'd think this might have served as a lesson to me, but, no, as you'll see, I made a habit of putting my foot in it on set – or not putting my foot in it, as in this case.

My next memorable adventure was two weeks on the famous Burton-Taylor epic historical drama *Cleopatra* (1963), which became the highest-grossing film of that year. Not because of me, I hasten to add. Again, my legs were involved but this time more to my advantage. One scene required a lot of sturdy-looking lower halves to be visible in the background. We, the extras, were asked to strip down to show how good our pegs were. Now, I may not always have had the best body shape, but my legs have never let me down – probably from all the parachute jumps I did. Anyway, some of the bigger extras, who thought they were a shoo-in, were passed over because they had skinny legs, while I was there for the whole scene. I didn't get to work with Richard Burton on this as he joined the film later in Italy, but I did work with him on a later occasion, which we will get to. I couldn't believe I was getting paid for having good legs! I thought, this is the life for me. From this film on, the bug stuck with me and I tried to get as much work as I could, to build up my name.

Me and my legs, *Cleopatra* (1963)

SPRITE

Around this time, I also got into car racing. I did not like sitting around as you can probably tell. I'd bought an Austin-Healey Sprite by selling the top-of-the-range Ford that Marion had got as a perk for working at the company of the same name. She never forgave me. Funnily enough, I've only owned two new cars in my life. The other was a Ford, too – a drophead which was stolen twice.

I raced for two seasons in the Sprite, usually finishing eighth or ninth. I wasn't the greatest driver but the races were such a thrill – they became quite addictive.

No. FIA 66: 2632

By Authority of the Fédération Internationale de l'Automobile

INTERNATIONAL
Competition Licence issued by the
ROYAL AUTOMOBILE CLUB
for ENTRANT and/or DRIVER

ISSUED TO Frank C Henson
PERMANENT ADDRESS 254, Kensal Road
London
W. 10

★ FOR VALIDITY SEE OVER ★

Signature of holder
Born on 2-5-36 at Brighton

Date of Issue 16th March 1966
Expires 31st December, 1966

Chairman of the Royal Automobile Club
London, S.W.1

RAC licence, 1966

One day I was racing at Brands Hatch. I got chatting to a young driver called Roy James who already had a great reputation. James was certainly out of my league. He had a single-seater Brabham for a start – quite a prestigious motor. We had a brief chat.

'I'm racing at Cadwell Park, next week,' he said.

'I've raced there,' I told him.

'What's it like?'

'I had trouble on the very long bend.'

'Oh.' That was the end of our conversation. He became famous but unfortunately not for his racing. In 1963 he was convicted for his part in the Great Train Robbery, and sentenced to 30 years.

Racing the Austin Sprite at Brands Hatch, 1965

In 1962 I worked on *The War Lover*, which starred Steve McQueen. It wasn't one of his best-known roles, but I got the opportunity to chat to him a few times on set. I knew he was a bit of a racer, and he would become known for it in his films like *Bullitt* (1968). Although he did many of his own stunts, he didn't do the famous motorbike jump over the fence in *The Great Escape* (1963) – he crashed attempting it – and the filmed jump was done by his stunt double, Bud Ekins. McQueen raced Minis at that time.

He told me his concerns about a female competitor he'd come up against. He was concerned she might kill someone with her driving, and I seem to remember reading that she did, a couple of years later.

EXTRA SPECIAL

You never stop learning in this industry. My best advice to people who want to get into the game is to try and become an extra first. I did it for four years from 1961 to 1965. Working as an extra – or just being on a film or TV set – is a great training for anyone who wants to go into stunt work. I learned about the camera, and when you can do this or do that. I talked to other extras and stuntmen. We made lots of notes. I messed up more times than I can remember but all the time you're taking things in, and you soon learn not to make the same mistakes twice.

A film set is an unforgiving place. People are under a lot of pressure to deliver on time and on budget. Everyone from the leading actors and the director to the second-unit assistant cameraman and the runners are expected to perform consistently well or their reputation will suffer, and they won't get asked back. It's a ruthless business, as is well known. It's easier to learn the fundamentals as an extra because you're not usually right in the middle of it. When you're a stuntman, you might be shadowing the lead actor or a supporting actor. Then you have to get it right or people will lose patience very quickly.

You'll see film extras who are understandably nervous and they won't think like an actor. But you have to. Here's an example. Imagine a scene in a film where you're one of many extras in a military unit, which is meant to march past the hero while he's delivering an impassioned speech. It's taken a long time for him to learn it, and the director has had to work out the most effective camera placements. He's discussed the camera movements with the director of photography. Then the weather's turned nasty and everyone has to wait around for hours, for a break in the rain or the wind. All this time the cost of employing the crew and other technicians is mounting. The producer is pacing up and down. He wants to see some action before he heads back to New York, so he can reassure investors that they're not wasting their money. Finally, the conditions are right. This might be the only opportunity to film this scene today. The actors are called to their starting positions.

The first assistant shouts, 'Action!' and the unit of extras is cued to begin marching. The leading actor starts his speech. Never mind that it will be overdubbed later, this is stirring stuff. You can hear the words clearly as you approach the platform on which he's standing. The speech sends shivers down your spine. You turn and smile at the hero who catches your eye and falters.

'Cut!' yells the director, who is watching the scene unfold on a monitor. 'I thought we told these guys to look straight ahead? Who is that idiot?' He means you. It starts raining. You've just ruined a day's filming. Under normal circumstances you've made a rookie error. But you are not working in normal circumstances. You're on a film set. You will not be asked back the next day.

Or there's a gunfight being filmed. Bang! Bang! Three extras get shot and fall back to the ground perfectly, as rehearsed. But two of them get up before the director calls 'Cut!' Guess which one gets kept on for another day's filming? You learn quickly if you want to carry on being a film extra.

STUNTMAN

After four years of being an extra I was ready for a new challenge. One day on set I had got chatting with some stunt guys. I was curious how they'd got into that line of work – it looked more exciting and like they were more involved in what was going on. When they found out I was an ex-Para and an amateur rally driver, they suggested I sign up with the Howard, Evans and Powell agency (HEP), which was the leading UK register of stuntmen at the time. HEP took a lot of ex-military men onto their books in the fifties and sixties, as the demand increased for ever more impressive and dangerous film sequences, requiring stunt actors. They welcomed me without much ado – I now had my foot in the door. As I mentioned earlier, all my experiences to date – in the military, working the Soho club doors, being an amateur racing driver – all proved to be fantastic training for the kind of career I was about to embark on. I have been a stuntman ever since and have met some of the top stunt boys in the country and all over the world. My racing experience was particularly useful – I became known as 'Frank the Crash' because of the number of cars I crashed (deliberately!) over the years – it must have been 40 or 50. I don't recall a time when I wasn't crashing cars on set.

As soon as you cross over from being an extra you notice differences in the way you're treated. You're more involved, more part of the production working as a stunt performer. I'm not knocking it, but as an extra you're one of the crowd – you'll all be in the same dressing room. As a stuntman you'll either share one with the stunt performers or you'll even have your own, if you're lucky. You eat with the cast and crew. In Make-Up you go to the front of the queue. You're given protective gear to wear, even if you're doing exactly the same as an extra. In the old days, as an extra you'd have to wait in line to get your chit signed before you got paid, whereas once I'd moved into stunts, the money was paid to me through my agent or straight into the bank. You were more of a part of things.

HEP AGENCY

I don't think it matters what you are in the industry – a writer, actor or director – you'll always need an agent to get on. They are the people who can get your foot in the door, and fight your corner when things go wrong. In the 60s the Howard, Evans and Powell agency (HEP) was the only place to go in London.

HEP was founded by three stunt guys – Frank Howard, Rupert Evans and Joe Powell. I'd met Howard a couple of times but sadly, he died; he was crushed by a horse in Morocco while filming. His wife Gabby really ran the agency after that.

There was a register for stunt performers. In 1965 there were about 65 people on it in total, but there was a core of 30 men and three women who were making a living from the work, as well as six or so stunt arrangers. Now there are something like 400 men and 150 women on the register. Peter Brayham and Peter Diamond were the two arrangers I worked with a lot. There was film work and TV work. TV work was popular because you'd get a fee for repeat broadcasting of any shows you were in, whereas films offered a one-off payment.

HEP was the only stunt agency going. Before they appeared, most of the men – it was mainly men – used for stunts were ex-military like myself, and they were treated just like film extras. It was thanks to Gabby and the rest that it became a respectable profession and we started to get paid properly for doing what no one else would do. HEP are an almost entirely forgotten footnote in film history now, which is sad, because they made a real difference to the working conditions of people like me, Vic Armstrong and nearly everyone else you'll see mentioned in this book.

THE 1960s

The Sixties were a great time to be living in London. They were also a great period for films and stunt performers. I was lucky to get into the Bond franchise pictures early on as well as working on some of the classic war movies from this time. To this day I still hear people saying that *Where Eagles Dare* is their favourite film of all time.

I made some great pals in the business early on who stayed friends for life. And to top it all my son, Franklin, was born in 1968. Yes, they were very good years.

CASINO ROYALE (1967)

As well as digging ditches in Shoreham, I also bought an E-Type Jag there. It was from the first year of Jaguars – 1961 – and it had the flat floor which is very sought after nowadays. A rich Scotsman – with a knighthood, I believe – had bought it. You had to be rich to buy one of these. He unfortunately died driving it, too. His blood was on the passenger seat and he'd obviously hit the windscreen. It was a write-off, although it still cost me £400. Little did I know how this wreck would help my stunt career. While racing Sprites, I'd got to know two brilliant panel beaters – Cyril and Lou Collins – who helped me restore the Jag in their garage. They also became very good friends over the years.

Now this car helped get me some work on a James Bond film. *Casino Royale* (1967) was actually a spoof of the Bond films, starring David Niven and Peter Sellers amongst others. The plot was that James Bond comes out of retirement to battle the evil SMERSH

Proud owner of an E-Type Jaguar

villains – a parody of the shadowy SPECTRE organisation from the original series of films.

Terry Yorke, the stunt arranger, told a mate of mine – Eddie Eddon – that they were looking for someone who could drive an E-Type Jaguar quite fast. Eddie, who was father to stunt performer Tracey who I worked with many times too, immediately thought of me and suggested that I'd be perfect. I was delighted when Eddie said they wanted to see me. Stunt driving was what I really wanted to do. The only thing they didn't tell me was that, for the purposes of the plot, the driver was meant to be a female. She was meant to be chasing James Bond, played by David Niven, who was driving an old Bentley.

In fact, they had a lady driver on set already, and she was good – probably faster than me. But I'd learned a bit about the film business by then. I knew one of two tricks. I knew, for instance, that directors liked everything to be larger than life. If you were pretending to hit someone, they didn't want to see a gentle slap, they'd want a full right hook.

So, when I went to audition I put some gravel on the ground, on a corner that the car was meant to skid on while executing a turn in the chase sequence. Then, as I approached the corner at speed, I hit the brakes and spun the wheel. The back of the car slipped around beautifully, scrunching the gravel and making a cloud of dust fly. As I thought, it looked bigger and better on-screen – just the kind of impact they were after – and I got the job. I did feel sorry for the lady, but that's the way the business works.

So now I was the main driver but there was a snag. For reasons I never fully understood, the wardrobe department insisted that I dress as a woman. I could understand wearing a wig and such, but the remit extended to putting on a miniskirt, just as my unfortunate predecessor had worn, and it definitely looked better on her.

Back in those days I could still be quite intimidated by the people on a film set so, like a fool, I went along with it.

'Hello, darling, show us your knickers!' shouted the crew as I walked on set. It was the kind of thing that people shouted in the sixties. I wouldn't stand for it now. I wouldn't have stood for it then had I realised that my bottom half wouldn't be seen in the film, and it really didn't matter what I was wearing below my shoulders. Thankfully, once I got to know the director for that sequence, he listened to my pleas and agreed that I could ditch the skirt.

Peter Brayham, who became a great friend and help to me in the business, happened to be watching as I made the sixth and only successful attempt to complete another difficult shot. I had to speed through a closing doorway – it was just as well he'd missed the first five attempts. Peter was so impressed with what he saw that he remembered me when it came to picking stuntmen for his next film. I've noticed so often that these little accidents of timing help build careers.

In the meantime, there's a sad coda to my E-Type Jag story. Having got me the gig in the first place, the production company asked me if they could buy it from me, so it could be used for a crash in the film. All Bond villains have to get their come-uppance, after all.

The producer said,

'We want to detonate a small explosion in it. If we blow it right up we'll give you £800 – how does that sound?' Since it had cost me £400 as a write-off, I jumped at the offer.

'Yeah, sure,' I agreed. 'Do a good job on it,' I urged Richard Talmadge, the second unit director. He grinned.

'Put another charge in,' he said to the technician.

'Boom!' Up went the Jag. It wasn't even a write-off anymore. I have regretted that decision ever since. If I still had the E-Type today, it would be worth well over £150,000. Ironically, the Jag I drove throughout the film was a later model – probably a 1965 model – which everyone assumed was worth more than my poor old 1961 original. Nevertheless, I did use the money to buy my next property, so it was hardly wasted.

ROBBERY (1967)

As I said, Peter Brayham remembered me when he came to coordinate the stunts on *Robbery* (1967), a film about the Great Train Robbery, starring Stanley Baker and directed by Peter Yates. Peter Brayham had me and Joe Wadham do all the driving. Joe drove his own police car on the film. I had to have my hair dyed blond for the part which cost £40 at Vidal Sassoon's – one of the top London salons. My wife would have done it for a fiver! This is strange because I remember every other aspect of the production as being low-budget and penny-pinching.

However, this film really made my name as a stunt driver, and driving is mainly what I did from then on, in my stunt career.

Steve McQueen saw and liked *Robbery* and, as a result, asked Peter Yates go out to Hollywood to make *Bullitt* with him. Unfortunately, I didn't get to go with him. It was a contrasting experience with *Robbery*, from what I heard. Instead of scrambling around, trying to find a spare tyre before the lead actors turned up on set, which was our experience on *Robbery*, there was no expense spared on *Bullitt* and it showed. It's one of McQueen's most highly regarded parts, and to his credit he did all the driving where he appears in close-up. The legendary Bud Ekins, together with Loren Janes, did the more dangerous long shots. But another happy consequence was that, after *Bullitt*, it became fashionable to have car chases in every film. It really is difficult to exaggerate just how many chases there were in the 70s and 80s. As a result, I never really stopped working after that, and you can trace the reason partly back to what I did on *Casino Royale*, which makes me proud. Maybe it was worth blowing up the E-Type after all.

YOU ONLY LIVE TWICE (1967)

In the same year I got to work on a real Bond film – *You Only Live Twice*. And I wasn't even driving in it. Dickie Graydon, of whom more later, got me the job as he knew the stunt arranger, Bob Simmons.

There's a famous sequence where Bond lets a small army of Japanese ninjas into Blofeld's secret volcano fortress. They slide down ropes from the volcano's false mouth to the dock below, where Blofeld is keeping stolen submarines. Leaving aside the unlikeliness of me as a Japanese ninja, this was one of the film's best and most exciting moments, and I was about to be in it. We had to rapidly lower ourselves from the studio ceiling to the ground. It was a long, long way down. Thankfully, help was at hand to shorten the experience, if only by a few seconds. One of the other stuntmen had obtained six of these special devices used by tree surgeons to allow themselves to move up and down quickly while working. If you watch the sequence carefully, you can see the six of us shoot down the ropes ahead of the others.

This film had an impact on me for a less savoury reason. We were meant to get £50 for each lowering, but when we started filming we were told we would only get £40 per attempt. One of the stunt crew decided we should strike over the £10 difference. As a result, the stunt coordinator, Bob Simmons, decided to sack the lot of us, and I didn't work for him for another 17 years. Things only changed with the intervention of Dickie Graydon who convinced Bob that I wasn't 'Frank the Crash,' but someone else. Once we were reacquainted, Bob and I became great friends, and he even came to stay with me and Marion from time to time. Misunderstandings can last a long time in the film business.

RICHARD GRAYDON

Richard, or Dickie as he was referred to by all who knew him well, was a lovely fella to be around and a great stunt performer. He had a wonderful and wicked sense of humour, one which always appealed to me. There's no doubt I wasn't in the same category as him professionally. He was a high fall man and had worked on many big films – both as an arranger and a performer – whereas I was always a stuntman.

To say he was fearless is an understatement. He was in demand for his ability to defy gravity – hanging on high above the ground. His most famous stunt was in Moonraker (1979) where he doubled Roger Moore in a fight scene a thousand feet above Rio, at Sugarloaf Mountain in Brazil. In the scene Bond is fighting with the giant henchman 'Jaws', on top of a cable car. He falls and then grasps the roof of the car. Dickie's left hand slipped off the roof and he held on with his right hand until he could regain a firmer grip. That was risky enough but, to add authenticity, Dickie did the scene without a safety harness. Talk about going above and beyond. He said later, 'It was the nastiest moment of my career.' My palms get sweaty just thinking about it.

We got on very well. He lived nearby and would come over for Sunday lunch. He was as entertaining and energetic at the table as he was in his work and in his regular letters to me. He pulled no punches when it came to slagging off all around him. He particularly loved to insult me. Though I had a great respect for Dickie, he could be very sour, because he could never understand how I and some of the other lads climbed the financial ladder while he didn't really, in spite of his professional accomplishments. Sadly, he died in 2014. Sunday lunches have never been the same since. God bless you, Dickie, you are very much missed.

WHERE EAGLES DARE (1968)

By 1968, I had become an established stuntman. I still lacked confidence, but I was known and valued as a stunt driver and performer. At this time Joe Powell – another great friend of mine and a well-known stunt coordinator – was getting lots of work in the war film genre and was putting together a big team of around twelve men, all ex-Army commandos. As you might have guessed, most of the villains in the war films back then were Germans. I dyed my hair blond and got a lot of German roles.

Joe was an ex-commando himself. He was going to take us to Austria to film *Where Eagles Dare,* a World War 2 action movie starring Richard Burton and Clint Eastwood. Just as we were about to set out the filming was postponed.

I was then offered a job by Joe Wadham on a film set in various European locations, called *Monte Carlo or Bust*. We were already in rehearsals when Joe Powell came back to me to say that *Where Eagles Dare* was now ready to film. I'm a man of my word, though, so I told him I'd committed to Joe. He was disappointed but appreciated the situation I was in. I later learned that, by turning the job down, I had missed out on meeting one of the greatest stuntmen in the world,

Asleep on the job?

Me and Richard Burton on the set of *Where Eagles Dare*, 1968

Yakima Canutt, who had worked on many classic films including *Stagecoach* (1939) and *Gone with the Wind* (1939). Yakima was the second unit director on *Where Eagles Dare*. He'd taught John Wayne practically everything he knew about stunts, including how to fall off a horse. What a legend. But that's life; I had kept my word anyhow. And all was not lost. I did get to do about a week on the film in the studios. I was on set with Richard Burton, who I'd managed to miss when filming *Cleopatra*. Burton was playing a British major John Smith, who was trying to escape to a rendezvous with an RAF plane. I was playing a German radio operator, one of the many troops he shot on the way to the airfield.

Back then, heavy drinking wasn't that unusual among leading actors, and Burton certainly drank a lot. On set, the producers would call out 'the quarterly', which meant lunchtime for the sparks and the camera crew. Burton would perk up and ask,

'Are the pubs open?' When the reply came back that they were indeed open, he would say, 'Then fuck your quarterly,' and rush offset, even though the break wasn't meant for the actors. I still wasn't terribly confident by then, and when he came back from the pub I was too intimidated to even ask, 'How was your drink?'

Incidentally, there was so much excellent stunt work on this film – including many dangerous stunts – that Clint Eastwood complained that the film should have been called, "Where Doubles Dare"!

A DANDY IN ASPIC (1968)

This was one of my most memorable HEP jobs – for good and bad reasons. It didn't even require a lot of stunt work. I had one scene as stunt double for Tom Courtenay, which involved driving a Cadillac at the actor Laurence Harvey. They had asked me to pick up Anthony Mann, the legendary director, from Gatwick Airport in the Cadillac. Also waiting were Tom Courtenay, Laurence Harvey and Peter Cook (best known for his comedy).

Rather than wanting to go straight to his hotel, as you'd expect after a long flight, Anthony Mann said to me,

'Come on, you can drive us to lunch.' When we got to the restaurant he insisted that I join them at the table. It was a great occasion, though I was too in awe of Mann to say much, which I deeply regret. I loved so many of his films – particularly *El Cid* (1961). Peter Cook dominated the conversation anyway, as I recall. Tragically, it turned out to be Anthony Mann's last film. He died of a heart attack during production and had to be replaced as director by Laurence Harvey.

MONTE CARLO OR BUST (1969)

This film was also known by its American title, *Those Daring Young Men in Their Jaunty Jalopies*. It was an interesting experience. There were six of us – me, Rocky Taylor, Joe Warren, Mark Boyle, Roy

Scammell, and Dinny Powell, who was one of my best pals and a pro-heavyweight boxer to boot. We were in Sweden, rehearsing our driving manoeuvres on ice and skid mats. There were no actors involved: we were to double them for the driving scenes, and then they would finish the film in the Rome studios. As a consequence, discipline wasn't as tight as usual, and we were free to get up to mischief.

In the Swedish mountains there was this hotel where they held a dance twice a week. Rocky loved it there so one evening we all went together. There was a group of Swedish skiing instructors, who seemed to be looking for trouble. I remember dancing, and this Swedish chap kept hitting me by wildly swinging his arms about. I let it go for a couple of times but then I hit him back. He then smashed a glass bottle, cutting the top of my eye. The dance exploded into a fight.

Most of the boys were around the corner from where I was, so I ran and yelled,

'Dinny, where are you? I'm fighting back here.' Dinny replied,

'I'm with you, Frank!' The boys came charging in and chairs, tables, and glasses were suddenly flying everywhere.

One of the bar staff shouted in English,

'Stop, we're calling the police!'

I could see we had to get out of there, so I opened up a window, shouted,

'Remember chaps, you're British!' and jumped. It was a 15-foot drop but thankfully there was plenty of snow. Everyone followed me out, sliding down the mountain. The incident made the local newspaper. They said we had smashed through the window but we most certainly hadn't.

GERT FRÖBE

Gert Fröbe, who I worked with on 'Monte Carlo or Bust', was a charming man. He's probably best known for his parts in Goldfinger and Chitty Chitty Bang Bang, as the villainous Auric Goldfinger and

Baron Bomburst, respectively. In real life he was the exact opposite. On Monte Carlo, Dinny Powell was doubling him as a German convict, while I doubled Peer Schmidt, who was playing a second German convict. Gert and I had many lovely conversations. In spite of his huge success, and considerable wealth, his life was overcast by the fact that his mother was in East Berlin and wouldn't leave. This was before the Berlin Wall came down, of course. As a pensioner she could pay to get out to the West, but her daughter and her grandchildren were still in East Germany, so she couldn't bear to leave. This was most upsetting for him, even if he could well understand the reasons for her staying put.

He was such a talented actor and great company. He could imitate the sound of any musical instrument with his mouth – it was uncanny.

Rocky Taylor, who was well liked by the hotel staff, said that we should pay £600 damages. I wasn't keen, as we hadn't started the fight, but in the end I think we all chipped in.

This was only the beginning of our troubles in Sweden. We were told not to go skiing but I went anyway and fell, damaging my knee. I can still feel the effects 50 years later. After my skiing accident, Dinny and I were in the car filming. We were playing German soldiers who had stolen some jewels. In the film, the Germans were speeding through the mountains when they turn a sharp corner too fast and lose a tyre, which rolls down the hill into a field full of reindeer. So, Dinny and I had to make our way down the steep slope, in the freezing cold, and hunt for the tyre which the crew had attached to the horns of one of the beasts. My knee was giving me terrible pain and the snow in the field was five feet deep, which didn't help. Dinny fell down a hole and yelled,

'Frank, get me out of here!' I replied,

'How can I? I can hardly walk.'

And all of this ended up in the film. We were there for five or maybe six weeks – a great experience.

Me with director Ken Annakin and a lot of bull, *Monte Carlo or Bust*, 1968

Incidentally, later we were filming in Monaco and, on a day off, I was sunbathing on the set. I opened my eyes and Grace Kelly – Princess Grace of Monaco – was standing a few feet away from me with two of her children. I probably thought I was dreaming but she had brought them to look at the model cars we were driving. Grace Kelly really was a beauty and had that star quality which is so hard to define, but all the Hollywood greats had it. It was sobering years later, when I was back in Monte Carlo, to drive past the corner where, in 1982, she had suffered a stroke and lost control of her car. The car had plunged down a mountainside and she had suffered fatal injuries as a result. She was only 52 years old. A tragic loss.

FRANKLIN

In 1968, my son Franklin was born and my life was changed forever. Marion had come out to Italy heavily pregnant, while I was filming

Monte Carlo or Bust. Dinny Powell took it upon himself to escort her everywhere by the arm. He kept telling me,

'For God's sake, stop her running around.' Easier said than done, as I can vouch to this day.

Anyway, we got back to London in time for the birth, at St Mary Abbot's Hospital in Kensington, just over the road from where we lived at the time. I couldn't have been more delighted when we had a boy. I couldn't help myself – I was thinking maybe he'll grow up to be a stuntman like me. Little did I know how true that was and what a brilliant stunt coordinator Franklin would become.

Of course, with me and Marion flying off all over the place, we wanted to get him settled in a school somewhere, so his life wasn't disrupted too much by my work. By the time he was five, I was desperate to get him into a good prep school. We tried a number of places, until we saw this place in Knightsbridge – Hill House – which was close to where we lived at the time in Kensington. It looked brilliant. Prince Charles had gone there at the same age as Franklin would, if he got in. It was run by a total one-off, a lovely old man called Lieutenant Colonel Townend.

I was nervous when I went to meet him, but I needn't have been. He really tried to put me at ease. He took a real interest in my life. When he found out I was a stuntman, he looked at me and, in a very cultured voice, said,

'Goodness. We've never had a stunt performer's child here before. We have Roger Moore's children and Mr Broccoli's grandchildren here. Do you know them?'

I answered truthfully,

'I don't know them, but I have worked for both of them.' I was worried that, because I didn't know either of them socially, he might count that against me. I couldn't have been more wrong.

'Well,' he replied, 'we had better get Franklin in, then, that will be most interesting.'

Franklin, stunt performer in the making

As I left the school building I reflected. Here's me, a boy from the Whitehawk estate, and I've just got my son into one of the top prep schools in the country. I couldn't have been prouder. For the next five to six years my son was very happy there. They had a different outlook to most other schools at the time. They emphasised the need for self-discipline and good manners, but they also made the happiness of the child their priority. They saw it as their mission to find out the child's talent and develop it. To that end they encouraged a wide range of physical activities – including Alpine pursuits and rifle shooting – alongside the usual academic ones. Franklin would be the first to say that was just as well. Looking back, it was a great early grounding in some of the skills he would need to get onto the stunt register. They certainly brought out the best in my boy. If only more schools had that approach.

THE 1970s

The 70s are widely acknowledged to have been a golden era for film and TV – perhaps the last truly great decade for the movies. There were all sorts of controversies. The level of violence in films became a running story in the newspapers, and I worked on one of the most notorious films of the decade – *Straw Dogs*. I also worked on most of *The Sweeney*, the British TV crime series which was considered beyond the pale at times. Of course, it looks very tame today!

It was also the decade when special effects (SFX) really took off and became an art form. I was lucky enough to be briefly involved with *Star Wars – A New Hope*, which was the first of a new line of blockbuster movie franchises which would come to dominate the business, and which used the new digital SFX to great effect.

Finally, the 70s were the swansong of a great many movie legends like Steve McQueen and John Wayne, who gave me some of the proudest moments of my career.

I think the 1970s was, in many ways, my favourite decade. My biggest films were in the 1980s but so much had gone right for me at this point. I had a beautiful wife and a young son who was attending Prince Charles's old school. We lived in a stunning mews house in Kensington and had a weekend cottage in Sussex. Work was regular and challenging. I thought back to my humble beginnings and thought, 'God, I've kind of made it.'

STRAW DOGS (1971)

Bill Cornelius was the stunt coordinator on *Straw Dogs*, a violent psychological thriller starring Dustin Hoffman and Susan George. He sent me down to St Ives in Cornwall to work on the film.

It was a great experience but I didn't get off to a great start with the director, Sam Peckinpah. I had just finished a fight scene, which had gone brilliantly. The crew applauded and Peckinpah even said,

'Frank, where were you when we were making *The Wild Bunch*? We could have used you.'

Stupidly I said,

'I was most likely out of work.'

Everybody laughed except Peckinpah. From that moment forth he clearly had the hump with me. Lesson number one in the movie business – don't try and be clever with the director, it'll get you nothing but grief. Many directors have massive egos – it's a necessary part of the job description – and they do not like being undermined or outshone in any way. To them it's like losing control of the set. Me and my big mouth.

IIIIIIIIIIII

He was annoyed with me on the next stunt I did, too, though this one certainly wasn't my fault – well, I would say that, wouldn't I? It was another gore-filled scene with the local villains attacking the cottage that Hoffman and Susan George were trapped in. My job was to get killed convincingly by a shotgun. I had this protective coat on that was filled with blood packets. The SFX team had come up with a new idea: an exploding gas canister would propel me backwards, mimicking the effect of a shotgun blast. Understandably I was a bit nervous, as this would be the first time I had experienced it. I was standing there, very clearly waiting for the canister to go off. Peckinpah yelled out,

'Frank, you're anticipating it!' but then the canister went off anyway. Fake blood went everywhere, all over the actors and me.

The director was not happy. Luckily the SFX team had prepared six coats for me, but it took hours to clean up the other actors before we could go again. At the second attempt I got it right – even Peckinpah couldn't complain.

It wasn't just me who got into trouble on *Straw Dogs*. Peter Brayham was having a joke with a producer who got so angry that he grabbed Peter's coat and chucked it into a fire. Peter went mad:

'What are you doing? That coat belongs to wardrobe!'

The producer sprang into the fire to save the remains of the coat. It was ironic given that their row was about the need to save money by cutting back on production costs.

ONE OF OUR DINOSAURS IS MISSING (1975)

(directed by Robert Stevenson)

Peter Diamond contacted me about doing some driving on this spy caper which starred Peter Ustinov and Helen Hayes. The plot involved microfilm being hidden in the bones of a museum dinosaur. The dinosaur is then stolen and ends up on the back of a truck being chased around the English countryside by three nannies. It was better than it sounds.

The film was made at Pinewood Studios and on location around Windsor and Holyport, in Berkshire.

Peter warned me,

'I'm not sure that you'll get the job as Pinewood have already got someone who does a lot of driving, but come down and we'll see if we can get you in.'

When I saw the chap in action, I said to Peter,

'No disrespect, but if I can't drive the skeleton around faster than that, I might as well give up stunt driving here and now.'

I got the job when they saw what I could do.

This was another job when I had to get dressed up as a woman. I think it was simply that there weren't that many stuntwomen back in the day – it's a different story now which is progress, in my view.

It was funny, though. I was getting ready to drive the truck on location one morning. A milkman was doing his shift and approached me from behind.

'Alright, lady, what's going on here?' he asked. The cameras hadn't been set up yet, so it wasn't obviously a film set. I turned around to him and said in my deepest voice,

'I'm no lady.'

'Blimey, you had me there,' he said, nearly losing his milk.

I was working with Dorothy Ford, who I adored, and her lovely sister Shirley Dent, who was mother to the great Stevie Dent. We were all dressed up as old ladies, to double the nannies. I was doubling for Helen Hayes. The two of them – Dorothy and Helen – didn't always get on, so the atmosphere could be a bit chilly when we were all driving together, and not just because we were filming in England. This was the first time that I took Franklin to a film set I was working on. There I was dressed as a lady, and there were more dinosaurs. God only knows what impression it made on him, though he still remembers being introduced to the great Peter Ustinov.

***One of Our Dinosaurs is Missing*, that's me driving on the left**

DOROTHY FORD

I have many lovely memories of this lady. Sadly, she is no longer with us. Dorothy was a legend in the stunt world and loved by everyone. She was probably best known for doubling six Bond girls but she also worked on the original Batman franchise in 1989, and Robin Hood: Prince of Thieves. In fact she accumulated over fifty stunt credits as well as six straight acting credits. She had a lot of bottle and there wasn't much she wouldn't do for the production she was working on.

Dorothy Ford, on location in Gibraltar for *The Living Daylights* (1987)

Dorothy was married three times and she held spectacular parties, mainly at Christmas and New Year's Eve. I was invited to many of them. In fact, I used to joke with her that I'd probably been to more of her parties than any of her husbands. Her other love was the white German Shepherd dogs which she kept. And champagne. She loved a glass or two of the fizzy stuff. A real lady and a real professional who it was my privilege to know on and off set.

BRANNIGAN (1975)

This is, without a doubt, one of my career highlights. *Brannigan* is a British thriller about an American detective (John Wayne) who is sent to London to extradite an American mobster – by fair means or foul.

Peter Brayham thankfully got me in to do some of the driving. The film, also starring Richard Attenborough and directed by my old pal Douglas Hickox, contains one of the all-time great car chase sequences. It includes a jump across London's iconic Tower Bridge which I was proud to play a part in. The sequence also unexpectedly landed Peter in jail, even if just for an hour, as I shall explain.

John Wayne was my all-time hero in the movies. Like millions of kids I would watch his films in the cinema, and then go out and play 'cowboys and Indians' for hours on end with my friends. I never thought in my wildest dreams that I would one day get to work with the big man – or Duke as we all knew him.

His real name, of course, was Marion Mitchell Morrison, and he was of Scottish-Irish descent. So we had something in common. I was such a fan that I managed to get tickets to the London premiere of *The Alamo* in October 1960. This was before I'd even started working as a film extra. It became one of my favourite films of his. When we arrived at the premiere I went to buy some drinks. While I was at the bar my wife met John Wayne who was standing with another great American actor, Gary Cooper. She asked Wayne for his autograph. Unfortunately, he didn't have a pen on him, so he asked Gary Cooper but neither did he, so Marion didn't get his signature. If someone had told me then that I'd be doubling him one day in a movie, I'd have laughed them out of the room.

Before he arrived on the *Brannigan* set we were all warned not to talk to Wayne. Some directors and producers are paranoid about the crew talking to the stars of the film, in case they upset them in some way. But after about a week or so Wayne turned around and said,

'Something wrong here? Why does no one want to talk to me?'

Someone explained, 'We've been instructed not to.'

'Well, that's fucking ridiculous!' came the reply. And we all fell about laughing. After that the atmosphere on set was great.

On another occasion Dougie Hickox thought he'd wind Duke up a bit. In his very refined accent he said,

'We know you are of Scottish-Irish descent – does that mean you hate the English?'

John Wayne turned and grabbed him by the throat.

'Well, kid, if I do, you'll be the first to know.'

It was brilliantly timed. The Dougie's reaction was priceless – for a moment he thought Wayne was serious. Still makes me grin to think about it.

I was nervous when we came to film my first driving sequence with him. Especially when he told me off after my first attempt. The shot was of me driving at Wayne at high speed, while he tried to shoot me. The director had told me to drive towards Wayne, swerving from side to side to evade the bullets, but also to kick up a lot of dust which always looks good. Wayne was not happy as he thought it looked false. He told me,

'Kid, that was terrible, I didn't know which way you were going to go, I was waving the gun all over the place.'

He told me to go in a straight line at him for as long as possible, then he could predict where I would end up, so that's what I did. It must have taken nerves of steel on his part because I was driving at least 70 mph and I swerved sharply to avoid him at the end. When the scene was finally done to everyone's satisfaction he said to me,

'That was great, kid.'

That was a really proud career moment.

As you can see from the photo, John Wayne and me are not exactly twins, but that didn't prevent me being his double for the amazing car chase scenes in *Brannigan*. All I needed was the same jacket, tie and shirt.

Doubling John Wayne – one of my proudest moments

It was a driving day. I was standing just behind Duke when a cameraman shouted, 'Hold it, gentlemen!' We both turned around and a flashbulb went off. The expression on the Duke's face is surprise but it is still one of my favourite photos.

I was driving a canary yellow Ford Capri, which was hot off the production line. Duke was going to be filmed in the close shots, of course, so he needed a few practise attempts to familiarise himself with the right-hand drive and also the stick shift. We filmed the main part of the chase in and around the Wandsworth area of London.

The chase sequences, through Battersea and Wandsworth, were choreographed by Peter Brayham. Never let it be said that Peter lacked drive and ambition. The climax of the chase was to include Brannigan jumping over a half-lowered Tower Bridge. The big 'gag' in the chase was the coupe landing with a crash on the other side, on a rubbish skip, with its boot open. It gave us quite a lot of bother. We had a meeting with the local authorities to discuss what we could and couldn't do on the London landmark. I remember John Wayne's son Michael, who was an executive producer on the film, being there, as well as Douglas, Peter and myself and one of the film's other producers. The Sunday before, I'd gone with Franklin to sit in one of the towers to watch them raising and lowering the bridge. This was a thrill for Franklin who was only eight years old at the time. We'd noted that both sides of the bridge could be raised and lowered independently, so at the meeting we explained that, to do the stunt safely, I'd need the second half lower than the first. They said this could be done. The meeting dragged on and on. In the movie business you get used to waiting around, but generally you make decisions pretty quickly, so this was frustrating. However, in the end they agreed to everything we wanted and we went away happy. We were all set up to film on the bridge when we heard back from them again. They'd had another meeting behind our backs and decided that we couldn't do the jump after all. They pretty much told us, we don't mind if you kill yourself doing the stunt but you're not damaging our bridge one bit. This really got Douglas Hickox's hackles up. He didn't like being told he couldn't do something.

Peter was driving a pale Jaguar – the villain's car in the sequence – the one that's being chased by Brannigan. Dougie told him to ignore the instructions from the authorities and carry on with the sequence. So he got in his car and crashed through the barrier at the entrance to the bridge. When he stopped the car there was almighty confusion. The authorities were furious and Peter wasn't backing down so it all turned into a bit of a shouting match. The police were on hand for safety reasons and, in the end, they nicked him, bundled him into the back of their car and took him back to the station. He spent an hour in the nick. When John Wayne turned up in person to secure his release, it more than made up for this indignity. Well, if John Wayne walks into a police station demanding his boy is set free, it's only going to end one way, right? Peter was out and had another great story to tell.

In the meantime we still had to finish the chase scenes and, after more heated negotiations, they agreed to let us complete the sequence on the bridge. Obviously they weren't going to let me do the same thing as Peter so we had to work out another way to make Brannigan's jump look convincing.

They allowed us to put the bridge back up as it had been for Peter's 'jump'. I carefully drove the car to the top edge and then reversed it down at speed, all the time looking ahead, which isn't easy to do, believe me. Then we moved over to the other side and I reversed up to the top edge before driving the Ford down at speed and crashing it onto a skip. Then they filmed John Wayne kicking the door open. We used a model for the long shot of the Ford crossing the gap, and a seven-foot rostrum to film the brief shots of the Capri in the air. In editing, they reversed the first shot – of me actually reversing back down the bridge to make it look like I was going forward. The magic of the movies! I must say it worked really well on-screen. Considering how primitive the technology was compared to what's available today, it still looks brilliant. The Duke signed me a photo afterwards with the words, *Next time we will jump it Frank, Good Luck, John Wayne.*

'Next time we will jump it Frank.'
Signed picture from my movie hero, John Wayne

The other major action set piece in the film was a great punch-up in The Lamb Tavern in Leadenhall Market. John Wayne had put his stamp, literally, on many of the classic western bar room brawls, so when the idea came together, the stunt boys were queuing up to be involved. Peter had worked out a routine. He made sure as many of the stunt guys as possible had cameos in the scene getting thumped by John Wayne.

As a stunt performer, being able to put that on your CV, backed up with footage, would do you no harm at all.

Even Peter said, 'I'm having some of that,' and got punched a couple of times. Nosher Powell was in the thick of it and got his fair share, too.

Alf Joint suggested to Peter that they set up a shot of Alf receiving a punch from Duke and sliding down the bar.

The Brannigan stunt team with the great John Wayne

'It would be like a homage to his western fights,' Alf suggested. Dougie Hickox agreed and the scene was set for Alf to get thumped. It was done in two takes. The punch itself took Alf onto the bar, then he slid down to the other end. No wires were used – Alf did it really well.

It was a great experience, and also good to have so many good stunt performers in the same scene at one time.

Dougie Hickox, John Wayne, Peter Brayham and me

JOHN WAYNE

I had many great conversations with John Wayne while I worked with him on Brannigan. It was most definitely a highlight of my fifty-year career in stunts. I discovered that Wayne had a love of dogs just like myself. When he was young he would take Duke, his Airedale Terrier, everywhere he went. A farmer who noticed this decided to call him Little Duke, and that's how he got his nickname.

I had to ask him about The Quiet Man, in which he played a bare-knuckle boxer who falls in love with Maureen O'Hara. It's one of my favourite John Wayne films. In the story her brother, played by Victor McLaglen, does not approve of the affair and they end up having one awesome punch-up that lasts for ages. I said him,

'That was a great fight sequence you did with Victor McLaglen.' He replied,

'You know, kid, Victor was 64 at the time and he wasn't a well man.' He went on to explain that a few stuntmen had been used for the scene – including John Ford's son, Patrick. They'd exaggerated the punches to make the fight look more dramatic. A real prizefighter, which Wayne's character had been, would have used short, sharp punches, but instead they took great swinging blows. It was typical of him that he wouldn't take credit unless it was fully due. What a great film, though, one of John Ford's best which is saying something.

Duke always carried little cards around with him. On the front was his name, John Wayne, and on the back his signature printed on the card. He would go around giving them out to anyone who asked for his autograph. One day on set I asked him,

'Why do you do this, Duke?'

He replied in his distinctive accent, 'Well, kid, you gotta remember that these people pay your bills.'

What little fame I have comes largely from my work on the Star Wars franchise. Believe it or not, I still get a lot of fan mail for my small

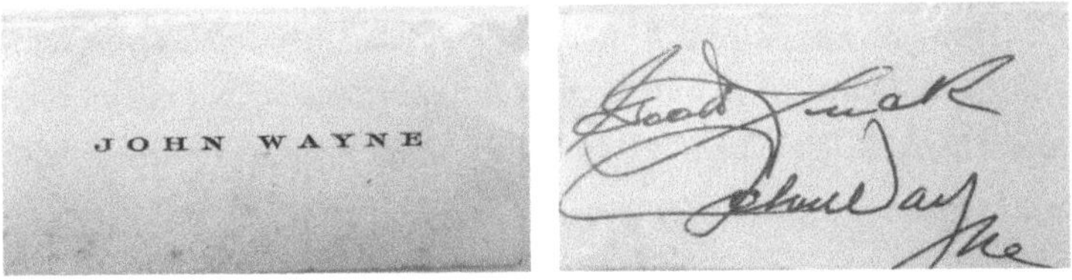

John Wayne's signature card – one of my most treasured possessions

contribution to those movies and I always respond, because if it's good enough for John Wayne, it's certainly good enough for me.

This reminds me of a story about another famous person, who shall remain nameless. I was working on his latest video. The story was that the star had escaped from prison. I had to chase him through a crowd and onto a stage. I was dressed in a policeman outfit and had two German Shepherd dogs with me. After the show, two of the girls who supplied the dogs asked me if I could get them the star's autograph. I said,

'Yeah, sure, I'll get it for you.' I went and asked him and he replied,

'Speak to my secretary.'

I thought that this was a bit arrogant of the man. If someone as accomplished as John Wayne could make the time for his fans, then why couldn't he? I did put the request to his secretary, but I don't know if the two girls ever got their autographs.

I was very saddened to hear of John Wayne's death in 1979. He was in many ways the last of a generation. He had firm ideas about what he stood for – not only as a man, but also what he represented in the American characters he portrayed on the big screen. I remember a story that, in The Shootist, the late western he made with Don Siegel in 1976, his character was meant to shoot someone in the back. Duke refused to do it.

'Whatever the cause,' he is reported to have said, 'I would never shoot anyone in the back. It's unthinkable for my image.'

He was always aware of giving his fans what they wanted from him. Duke was a pleasure to talk to, a great American icon and my all-time movie hero. He left us an awesome legacy of work. I'm very proud to have worked with the great man.

THE SWEENEY (1975-1978)

This British TV crime series is still very well regarded to this day, probably due to the brilliant on-screen chemistry between the two leads – John Thaw and Dennis Waterman. They played the errant, put-upon Flying Squad cops, Detective Inspector "Jack" Regan and Detective Sergeant George Carter, respectively, who were always getting into violent tussles with London villains. I was one of three people playing, among other parts, Regan's driver 'Bill' – though this was never acknowledged in the credits. Tony Allen and Peter Brayham were the other two behind the wheel of that Bronze Consul GT, depending on the schedule.

John Thaw was a very fine actor. He had the crew convinced that he was a cockney for a while, even though in reality he was Manchester born-and-bred.

On my first day's filming I was driving over Hammersmith Flyover, doubling John Thaw, with Dennis Waterman sat next to me. I could tell it was going to be a hit – their banter was terrific. Dennis did confide to me early on that he thought the show would be short-lived, but thankfully he called that one wrong. He, of course, went on to even greater success in *Minder*, where he played the straight man to George Cole's wheeler-dealer.

Peter Brayham was the main stunt arranger on the show and, when some fighting and a bit of reckless car driving was called for – which was pretty much every show – he would get me in. He knew that I could handle a car pretty well, so he would get me to assist with the crashes and turnovers. We ran through everything first so we knew where we were going. Peter would say,

'We're doing it half-speed' for the run-throughs. Well, film was expensive in those days – you didn't want to turn over until you had rehearsed the sequence at least once. The manoeuvre I remember best took place in Battersea. I had to turn a car over as I hit a brick wall. As I did this, the wall actually came down, making it look even better than we had planned. Everyone was pleased and I'm sure me and Peter took all the credit.

With John Thaw and Dennis Waterman, *The Sweeney*, 1978

Peter choreographed the fights so well that they looked real – not staged at all. As with most TV series, we had very limited time to film on location, so Peter's expertise was invaluable for making sure we came in on time. Back then the villain's choice of tool would be a baseball bat. Peter would make sure that all the gangs in *The Sweeney* carried bats with them. He insisted that us stuntmen wore extra padding as we got hit for real with the bats – no one argued with him about that.

By then, Peter and I had this unspoken understanding. He would bring me in and tell me what he wanted and I got it straightaway. He didn't have to explain at length. He knew what I was capable of and I knew what he liked. Some people found Peer a bit loud, but he was almost always right and what he said was worth listening to. He talked the talk and produced the goods on-screen. His motto was, 'You don't take risks, you eliminate them.' That's why so many directors and producers wanted him on their projects, and why stunt actors jumped at the chance to work with him. Peter was very good to me and got me a lot of film and TV work over the years.

One of my highlights on *The Sweeney* came near the end, in 1978. It's difficult to explain to young people just how popular Morecambe and Wise were in their day. They were comedy superstars, and their Christmas TV special was one of the most eagerly awaited media events of the year. They were one of the first productions to have people on from other channels and shows. It probably sounds old-fashioned now, but everyone used to tune in to see who their special guests would be.

Morecambe and Wise were good friends with *The Sweeney* lot, having invited them on to do a comedy sketch in their 1976 Christmas Special. So it was great when they returned the favour and agreed to appear in an episode of *The Sweeney* – as themselves. Even better, I was Eric Morecambe's double – that's me standing next to the great man in an oversized flat cap and wearing a Luton Town scarf – his beloved football club.

The Sweeney with Morecambe and Wise

The last time I saw John Thaw he was working on his hit show, *Inspector Morse*. Tony Allen, who had been a tailor to many of the boxers and gangsters I met in the sixties, had become great mates with John. He had been wardrobe master on *The Sweeney*, as well as sometime driver 'Bill', and had followed John onto *Morse* to be head of wardrobe again. We were chatting in-between takes, and I said to John,

'Tony made me a beautiful coat thirty years ago.' Quick as a flash John said,

'And Tony reckons you're still wearing it now.' His timing was great and we all had a good laugh at my expense!

PETER BRAYHAM

I met Peter at a party one night. We'd been introduced before but this was the first time we had really talked. I was there with Marion and Peter was in the corner of the room with a bunch of weightlifters. Don't ask – these things happen in show business.

During the evening one of the weightlifters was coming on strong to Marion, so I went up to him and said,

'Keep that up, and you'll be in trouble.'

I kept an eye on him after that, and later he wandered over to me and said,

'You wanna stop looking at me, it'll do you no good.' Before he could finish his sentence I belted him and he hit the floor. Peter came up to me and said,

'Right, my friend, this could get you in a lot of trouble.' I replied,

'Go on, then, show me. See what good it does you.'

Well, what can I say? It was like a scene straight out of The Sweeney! We became great pals from that time on. I think he realised that I could handle myself in a fight, which I had learned to do while working on the doors. I must stress this again, though: I am not proud of fighting and it has not been my way for a very long time. My temper is still there but that's only because of my background, I guess. I would advise anyone to avoid a fight if they can, as it most certainly does take the bigger man to walk away.

Peter Brayham and me in costume.
Chance encounter with John Thaw in London

Peter was a great storyteller. He could really hold people's attention. You could hear a pin drop while he acted out all the parts and dragged you into a story.

I remember one time he was on a picture with the Boulting brothers, who were very posh in that peculiarly English way. They had stopped shooting for the afternoon to watch the cricket. Peter, who was very good with accents, rang up the wardrobe master and pretended to be the director.

'Now look here, Duncan, I need the Humpty-back waistcoats for the dwarfs this afternoon. Can you fast-track them for me?'

There was a long pause on the end of the line, followed by Duncan saying, 'Humpty-back what? We haven't had any requests for them… Today? How many do you want?'

Peter knew he had him good and proper so, still in character, he said, 'Look, I don't care how much it costs, just get them here this afternoon!' Peter hung up.

Two hours later, Duncan came rushing into the room where Peter and the Boulting brothers were still watching the cricket. 'Gentlemen, I can't get those Humpty-back waistcoats to you on time; the dwarfs will have to go without.'

Roy Boulting looked up from the television and shouted,

'Someone call a doctor, this man's obviously fucking mad!'

Finally, I remember Peter giving me a job on a period costume film with Joan Collins. I was playing one of the thugs who were robbing a stagecoach. We had to get the passengers out of the stagecoach, line them up and then take their purses and jewellery.

My single line was to say,

'There's no purse on this one.'

I said it with this rather posh accent that I had developed, and the director shouted,

'Cut! You can't say it like that.' So, we did about three takes and I still couldn't say it in the rough manner he wanted. On the fourth take, Peter put a purse in my hand as I said it. Everybody cracked up – except the director and Joan Collins, who didn't look very amused. It was so typical of Peter.

The director said,

'I suppose you think that's bloody funny.'

Peter returned, 'Well, it's a comedy, ain't it?' So we went again and I got it perfectly, with just the rough voice he wanted. How I did it, I don't know, but Peter had broken the tension at just the right time and that probably helped.

Not everyone liked him. A wardrobe mistress once said to me, in a broad Glaswegian accent, 'Your pal, that Peter guy, he's not liked round here. He's gonna get stabbed by everyone.'

I replied, 'What, you mean like Julius Caesar?'

She looked at me over the top of her thin reading glasses and said, 'It won't be as discreet as that!'

Unfortunately for Peter, he was a lifelong smoker – cigarettes in the early days and cigars later on. I remember travelling with him somewhere. The car was so full of cigar smoke I could hardly see out of the windscreen or breathe.

I said to him, 'Peter, for fuck's sake put it out, it's killing me.'

Peter turned and replied, 'It's killing you? What the fuck do you think it's doing to me, then?' He died from a heart attack in 2006 – a deeply missed colleague and dear friend.

AT THE EARTH'S CORE (1976)

I worked for Joe Powell on this fantasy film about a prehistoric underground land where dinosaurs still roamed. But it was more notable to me for being the first film set which Franklin visited. I arranged for him and four friends to go to Pinewood on his birthday. He was about eight at the time. They all ran into the 'cave' where the big rubber dinosaurs were being kept, and then ran out screaming. It was very funny. It gave him the film bug, too.

SKY RIDERS (1976)

This film centred on the kidnapping of an industrialist's wife by terrorists, and then the daring attempt by a group of hang-gliders to rescue her from the mountaintop hideaway where she is being held. James Coburn plays the ex-husband who plans the rescue.

Unfortunately, the film made more of an impact because of what happened during production than for its cinematic qualities. There was a terrible accident. Three men, including me, were wearing fire suits for a stunt when there was a premature explosion and a fireball swept over our heads and exploded over the crew, setting some of them on fire. When I saw what was happening, I rushed over to help. The man who was most alight was the Greek boom operator,

Elias Panayotopoulos, and I tried to get his flaming T-shirt off him and extinguish the fire. He died five days later. Thoughts of this accident will haunt me as long as I live. It's a terrible irony that there were absolutely no problems with the aerial work, which was quite demanding, but that the tragedy occurred in that mundane time when everyone's hanging about waiting for the action to start. It goes to show that film sets can be dangerous places even when there's no stunt work going on. The film's producer was arrested, and an executive producer was detained for several weeks. Eventually they reached an agreement with the Greek government. Meanwhile filming carried on after a break of three days – the show must go on, regardless, it would seem.

On the set of *Sky Riders* with James Coburn

A better memory from *Sky Riders* was meeting the legendary French singer and actor, Charles Aznavour. He was a lovely man. We were filming in the desert in quite an inhospitable location. I asked him,

'Is your wife here?' He looked at me as if I could not be serious and said,

'I have an apartment in Paris and a villa in the South of France, why would I bring her here?' I didn't tell him that Marion was with me.

For the rest of the filming we were up in the mountains. I wasn't there to do any hang-gliding, but two of the American stunt gliders – brothers, I think – asked me if I'd like to go up with them one day. I told them I'd love to. It was brilliant. We ran off this mountain at 4000 feet and glided gently around, catching the air thermals. It was so peaceful up there. When we eventually came in to land, the guy I was with said,

'Start running!' My legs were going around like a Tom and Jerry cartoon but the landing was smooth. I would still love to do it again.

A final memory is of going for swim with the director, Douglas Hickox, on our crew break one day.

Doug turned to me after we had swum out quite a distance and said,

'Frank, do you realise we are now swimming in the Aegean Sea?'

I replied, 'Bloody hell, Dougie, I thought we were still in the Mediterranean! Is that how far we've come?'

But my lasting memory will always be of that poor young man.

R.I.P. Elias Pan-ayotopoulos.

On the set of *Sky Riders* with my best mate, Peter Brayham

STAR WARS – A NEW HOPE (1977)

I think it's fair to say no one had a clue just what a massive blockbuster this film was going to be at the time. Peter Diamond, the stunt arranger, didn't. He went off to work on another film, leaving Reg Harding in charge. Pete and Reg were best friends. This was a lucky break for me because Reg phoned and asked if I could do a couple of weeks at Shepperton Studios. I accepted tentatively. We knew each other well from previous projects we'd worked on together.

The director was a friendly, animated young man called George Lucas. By the time of *Return of the Jedi*, George seemed under a lot more pressure – as I guess he was. From my view on the periphery, he looked less preoccupied, and more like he was just having fun on *Star Wars*. I suppose appearances can be deceptive.

Just to show that I, too, had no idea how big the film was going to be, I discharged myself after a week because there was a property auction I wanted to go to – I was seriously getting into property development at the time. I went to the auction for two days in a row but didn't end up with any of the houses I wanted. It was a wasted journey. I should have stayed on the film.

However, *Star Wars* did leave me with a permanent reminder of my brief time working on it. I was playing a storm trooper and five of us were involved in a couple of explosions. For the second blast, the special effects guy warned me and the other stuntmen,

'This is going to be a big one – make sure you keep your backs to it.' One of my colleagues ignored his advice and ended up with a cut in his eye. I ended up with a lump of cordite in my arse – it was there for about twenty years. It's safe to say I saved my best work for *Return of the Jedi*, of which more anon. I guess I'd also be entitled to say that my experience of *Star Wars* before *Jedi* was a pain in the backside!

THE PROFESSIONALS (1978–83)

QUADROPHENIA (1979)

The Professionals was another long-running British crime series, similar in many ways to *The Sweeney*. It focussed on the activities of a fictitious law enforcement operation, pitched somewhere between MI5 and MI6, which dealt with crimes beyond the remit of the police force, but below a level requiring military intervention. Peter Brayham was the stunt arranger. He got me in to do a lot of driving, of course, and I also played a couple of heavies.

It's easy to forget how massive these TV shows were back in the day. *The Professionals* regularly got viewing figures in the millions, but this was before home computers and cable TV let us watch anything at anytime. Instead, in Britain we had a choice of three TV channels, or a trip to the local cinema. Like *The Sweeney*, the series relied heavily on the charisma of the two lead actors – Lewis Collins and Martin Shaw. Both were lovely men, and very different characters in the series as well as in real life. Lewis was the cheeky extrovert, William Bodie, while Martin played the more sombre Ray Doyle. The famous Scottish TV actor, Gordon Jackson, played their boss, the dour George Cowley. That's another thing about that era – you rarely saw actors cross over from TV to film – they were like separate worlds. The stunt guys, however, switched endlessly between the two formats.

In fact, this happened on *The Professionals*. There was a big British film in production at the time. *Quadrophenia* was the movie of a rock concept album of the same name, by British legends *The Who*. It concerns the trials of a young Mod, Jimmy, who just doesn't fit into society at all. It was set in my home town of Brighton, so I was jealous when Peter Brayham went off to work on the film, leaving me temporarily as stunt arranger on *The Professionals*.

Thankfully, when the production team came to London, I also got to work on *Quadrophenia*.

I'll explain what I did but first I should say that having to manage the stunt guys on *The Professionals* gave me a newfound respect for Peter. Stunt performers can be a handful, I realised. Especially when I found myself in charge of them for the biggest episode ever recorded for the show. The police were at least helpful, locking down the backstreets while we filmed some chase sequences. The plot concerned a kidnapping, as I recall, and there were times when I wished someone would bundle me in the boot of a car and drive off.

I had so much aggravation. There were seven stuntmen to be coordinated – all driving and crashing cars, performing fights and other more challenging stunts. One of the guys, Romo, complained about his scene. He was meant to get shot and fall into a dirty canal.

'I don't want to do that – it's filthy,' he said.

'Romo,' I said, 'that's what I got you in for. It clearly says in the script that you get shot and fall into the canal. What did you think you were going to do?' Bless him, he did it in the end. Another man kept turning up late because he was working on another job – he was a friend, too. Working with these guys was a nightmare – is this what I was like? I wondered.

Cliff was meant to be up on a crane.

'I don't like height jobs – can we swap?' he asked.

'It's not going to be that high, Cliff,' I explained. 'The crane will be only be up 40 or 45 feet.' It was a simple job really, but I swapped with him simply to avoid any more aggro. I knew if Peter Brayham was there he'd have just said,

'Do it, or you're sacked.' But I wasn't like Peter, I was much more one of the boys. That probably explains why I wasn't put in charge very much, and that suited my personality better. I just liked to do a good day's work and leave the fussing to the people who were good at it.

Martin Shaw and Lou Collins were brilliant drivers, so they did quite a lot of their own scenes. I did Martin's more dangerous manoeuvres, while Peter doubled for Lewis. Even though I mainly doubled for Martin Shaw I became really friendly with Lewis Collins. Lewis was volunteering at the time for the 10 Para Regiment of the Territorial Army, so we had some experiences in common. He even passed initial selection for the 21 Special Air Service but was prevented from progressing because senior officers deemed him a potential security risk, on account of his celebrity. He used to go jumping with my son, Franklin, who really warmed to him, too.

Lewis was a lovely fella – really down-to-earth and always joking around with the boys. There was no side to him – he just enjoyed life to the max. He'd invite me to parties which could get quite out of hand, and the ladies always made a beeline for him. Sadly, he died in 2013 after battling cancer for five years. A big loss.

It was a relief when Peter phoned to say he'd got a part for me on *Quadrophenia*, even if it sounded like quite an odd role for me. They wanted me to play a postman. A stuntman – playing a postman? All was to become clear soon enough. No, I wasn't to get bitten by a dog. I had to accidentally crash my van into the lead character, as he drove his Lambretta scooter. My mate Colin Skeaping was the double for Phil Daniels' role and did a great job of skidding into the collision. As much as I enjoyed filming this sequence – it was a great stunt – the best bit came when I had to go to the studio and dub my dialogue on the film with Phil Daniels.

My line was 'Fifteen years I've been driving and I've never had an accident.'

Phil Daniels then goes ballistic at me,

'Never had an accident, you got me, though, didn't you? Mr Postman, fuck off!'

Come to think of it, it wasn't that different from being a stunt coordinator!

DRACULA (1979)

The final film I worked on in the 1970s was *Dracula*, where I was lucky to meet two of those legends I mentioned earlier, Laurence Olivier and Donald Pleasence. I can even say that I acted with them both, as this was one of those films where I had a proper credit: 'Demeter sailor!'

We were filming down in Cornwall again. Laurence Olivier was one of those people who could enter a room and silence it – he had immense presence and charisma. His stand-in knew me and introduced me to Larry. One day, I plucked up my courage and asked him, 'What was it like to work with Marilyn Monroe?'

He was gracious but made it clear that it had been a contrasting experience.

'Let's just say for the first three weeks I absolutely adored her,' he told me. Yes, let's just leave it there.

Me as 'Demeter Sailor' in *Dracula* – a rare acting part!

This was also one of the first times I met Eddie Powell, who was the stunt coordinator on the film. I had to fall down the stairs for one of the actors. Because Eddie and I got on so well, he hired me throughout the film.

IIIIIIIIIIII

I also had the pleasure of meeting Donald Pleasence. What an amazing actor he was. Like Gert Fröbe, he could send shivers down your spine while playing an evil character, but off-screen he was the nicest gentleman you could hope to meet. He also had a great sense of humour. It was a great way to see out the decade.

Another treasure possession: signed photo from Sir Laurence Olivier, who played Van Helsing in *Dracula*

THE 1980s

The 80s were an amazing time for me. I got to work on some of the biggest films of all time – including *Return of the Jedi* (1982) and *Indiana Jones and The Temple of Doom* (1984) – and do some hair-raising stunts, including probably the worst accident of my career. As a result of this accident, my short-term memory was impaired – my recall of recent events fell out with the stitches. Thankfully there have always been plenty of people to remind me of my exploits, and it certainly didn't stop me working.

Off-screen, my son Franklin came of age, ensuring the continuation of the Henson stunt dynasty, and my property portfolio progressed in leaps and bounds.

The British film industry shrank a bit in the 1980s – tax concessions which had attracted investment were cut, and cinema audiences were declining because of competition from the new video cassette recorders (VCRs – remember them?). As a result, most of the big-budget films I worked on were on location abroad. But I never minded that. Another consequence of the lack of inward investment was that smaller, independent production companies were formed, and some did very well.

Some of the most highly rated film and TV work in Britain was commissioned by the BBC, and the newly formed Channel 4. *Edge of Darkness* TV series (1985), which I worked on and which won loads of awards, was an example of this. It was broadcast to such critical acclaim, on BBC2, that the Beeb decided to repeat it on BBC1 shortly afterwards. The director of that series, Martin Campbell, is to this day one of my favourite people in the business. A real gent and brilliant director.

Special effects continued to develop at an amazing rate. One of the most notable examples was the werewolf transformation scene in *An American Werewolf in London* – another film I'm proud to have worked on.

I did lots of TV in the 80s – from *The Professionals* to *Casualty* and *London's Burning*. As you probably realise by now, I'd work on anything if the money was good and the job was interesting. As a result, there was never a dull moment for me in the 1980s.

THE LONG GOOD FRIDAY (1980)

Roy Alon, the stunt coordinator, was a lovely fella: a true Yorkshireman with a heart of gold. He would do anything for you. He'd got himself pretty busy with Vic Armstrong back in the day and built his reputation as a high fall man. Roy was another man who liked nothing better than hard work. He worked on over a thousand films before his untimely death in 2006. Incredible. *The Long Good Friday* is about the London criminal underworld and starred the late Bob Hoskins as cockney crime linchpin Harold Shand, trying to cut a deal with the American Mafia while fending off the IRA.

After working on *The Sweeney* and *The Professionals* for so long, the subject matter felt quite familiar. *The Long Good Friday* won loads of accolades – it's often in people's lists of favourite films of the 1980s. Incidentally, talking of *The Sweeney*, another pal of mine who had appeared in some episodes was also in this film. Brian Hall played Bob Hoskins' chauffeur Alan, though he'll probably always be best remembered for his appearances as chef Terry Hugh, in the BBC comedy *Fawlty Towers*.

Roy asked me to be involved in the stock car scene, which comes later in the movie. I'd done plenty of stunt driving by this time so he knew he could rely on me. We filmed at Hackney racetrack for a couple of nights. There were a few of us – Vic Armstrong, Billy Horrigan, Jim Dowdall and me – charging around a track with actual stock car drivers. As Jim said, the stock car drivers acted like they had a point to prove. Who were these flash stunt boys, coming here and taking over our track? We put in about 20 or 30 laps before they signalled the take. We headed for where we would have to bounce off each other – in the corners. Afterwards the stock drivers told us not to take the driving too seriously or they would be out of work, which we took as a compliment.

Getting thrown through a window in *The Long Good Friday*

There was, in the story, a shoot-out at the stock car race. Roy got me to double for the actor Tony Rohr, who was playing an IRA terrorist called O'Flaherty. Roy had a credited part, playing the IRA moneyman called Captain Death. O'Flaherty was to be shot and thrown out of the window, while Roy, as Captain Death, drove over my dummy and crashed into my car. It took a while to get the timing right, but it was good fun so no one minded. Having a good atmosphere on set makes all the difference, especially when the stunts are complicated. It's easier to concentrate when you're relaxed, though not too relaxed or you get careless.

My favourite contribution to *The Long Good Friday* was near the beginning of the film. I doubled Bob Hoskins' chauffeur, Eric (played by Charles Cork), in one of the film's iconic sequences. Eric drives Harold Shand's mother to Easter Mass. He walks out of the church and heads back to the motor to wait for her. When he puts his key in the ignition, the car is destroyed by a bomb exploding. Roy gave me the job because he knew I had a bit of bottle. He warned me,

'They're big, heavy explosions.' I said,

'Don't worry about it, I've been blown up a few times now.' I think I got paid a grand.

For the scene to have its full impact, I had to be seen in the car as the bomb detonated. The way it was filmed was genius. There were actually three explosions. With the first explosion, the boot gets blown off. On the second explosion the bonnet flies off. At that point they cut to a wider shot and I had to get out and run for cover as the car is blown to smithereens. The cut was so fine you never saw me getting out – it was brilliantly done. I learned on this film how the top editors earn their money. I was very proud of my work on it, too. And glad I got out of the car on time otherwise it could have been my last Good Friday – Roy wasn't joking about those explosions!

MARTIN CAMPBELL

I have worked with Martin Campbell for many years. You could never meet a more loyal or likeable director. And loyalty is a rare quality in the film industry. We worked together on the British TV detective series Shoestring, as well as The Professionals and Edge of Darkness.

He was justifiably proud of his TV work and used to say he'd resist the big bucks productions, unless there was something more to them. I used to wind him up on Edge of Darkness by saying, 'Martin, I bet

you end up in Hollywood.' He just had that calm authority about him that all the top directors seem to have, as well as bags of talent. Lo and behold, he is a well-known Hollywood director now, having done a couple of Bonds as well as The Mask of Zorro (1998) and The Legend of Zorro (2005). My son Franklin worked with Martin in his home country of New Zealand. At first Martin didn't realise he was my son but, as soon as he did, that was it, he took a liking to him.

Franklin was doing a stunt on a bridge and Martin shouted, 'Franklin, if you don't pull your finger out, we'll get your father out here!' Brilliant.

Martin used to live in the same area of London as me for a while, and always wanted to know why my house was bigger than his. I never let him forget it. Whenever Martin's in the UK he'll ask me to do something. He got me in to do a couple of days' work on the new version of Casino Royale (2006) starring Daniel Craig. That was an eye-opener – how things had changed since the first film with David Niven. It's always great to see Martin, such a lovely man, even if his house is smaller than mine.

GREAT EXPECTATIONS (1981)

The TV miniseries adaptation of the Charles Dickens novel was memorable for me mainly because of a near-death escape. Peter Brayham was the stunt arranger. It's not surprising that in all the years I've worked in the industry, I've had some hairy moments, and this was definitely one of them. I was doubling the actor Peter Whitbread, who was playing the part of Compeyson – the convict and fraudster who drowns in a fight with Magwitch. This was a case of life imitating art, as they say. I was in the water by this paddle steamer, and the cloak I was wearing was entangled in the rotating paddle. Each time it took me under the cloak got heavier and tighter around my neck and I was fighting to breathe. I was trying to yell, 'Stop!' but the crew was concentrating on the main filming action and I couldn't move my arms to alert them. I was losing consciousness when Peter looked up, saw me and stopped the filming in a flash. Otherwise there would have been no expectations for me.

Me and Dave Holland during filming of *Great Expectations*

AN AMERICAN WEREWOLF IN LONDON (1981)

Another iconic movie that I was lucky to work on. At the time it got a lot of publicity because of the amazing make-up special effects pioneered by the American Rick Baker – the transformation sequences were like nothing else at the time. It's aged well and is still highly regarded. John Landis, who had directed *The Blues Brothers*, was in charge, and Alf Joint was the stunt arranger. I was called in to do some driving for one of the climactic scenes in the movie. It's quite a famous scene where the werewolf jumps out into the traffic in Piccadilly Circus and causes mayhem on the streets. The London Transport Police were happy to cooperate but we had to keep the stunts very short. Because of the disruption that closing the streets would cause, we were only allowed to film at 4 in the morning in ten-minute bursts. So, we had to drive out, crash, then clear the road and get it reopened in ten minutes flat. It was the opposite of most on-set situations, where you're waiting around forever, trying to get everything exactly right before you start to film.

John Landis also performed one of the stunts, crashing through a bookmaker's window after being hit by a car driven by Vic Armstrong. Vic also had to drive a double-decker bus during the same sequence. The script called for the bus to slide, but everyone thought that the only way you could achieve that was using what were known as British transport skid pans – heavily watered areas on which bus drivers were taught to keep control of their vehicle in situations like driving over an oil slick, for instance. One of the special effects technicians, a lovely man called Dave Bickers, found an ingenious way to get the bus sliding. He attached smaller trolley wheels to the back of the bus's axle, allowing Vic to throw the wheel around and be sure that the back of the bus would skid round on cue. The finished scene only lasts minutes, but we had to film it over two nights to get it right.

MUD VERSUS CONCRETE –

Everyone assumes you'd prefer to turn a car over into nice, soft mud than onto hard concrete but it's not the case at all. At least, not for me. What happens is you come off a ramp, go over and stop dead in the mud. The car stops dead but your body doesn't, and that can be very dangerous. I prefer turning on concrete. There's a good chance that the car's going to slide on its roof which is better for the camera – but also for you inside the car.

IIIIIIIIIIII

RAMPS – Back in the 1980s I was hired to turn an engine over on London's Burning, the British fire-fighting TV drama. I got to the studios and my heart sank a bit because they'd build a wooden ramp – I suspected a fire truck full of water was going to need something more substantial to support it as it went over. Here's another thing. I prefer the ramp to be on the same side as the driver's wheel, but they'd rigged it to be on the passenger seat side. Most stunt drivers prefer that because they figure that – if the ramp's on the passenger seat side – then they'll be closer to the ground as the car turns, which is safer.

But I prefer going over the ramp with my driver's side wheel, because I can see the ramp more clearly and you're going to go higher up in the air and hit the ground harder. This means you'll get a bigger impact – more bang for your buck. I used to have a kicker at the top of the ramp that gives the front wheel an extra nudge to turn it over.

If you're rigging for yourself, you can take precautions. But when you're there and everything's set up for filming, you can't say,

'I don't want to do it.'

So off I went in my loaded engine and – sure enough – as the passenger side front wheel went up, the ramp collapsed under the weight. To be honest, I think I hit it badly, too. The truck didn't turn over.

Two weeks later they got a stunt pal – Gabe Cronnelly – in to do it again. They'd built a steel ramp this time and he nailed it – did a great job. These things happen.

STAR WARS – RETURN OF THE JEDI (1982)

This is without doubt the biggest movie that I worked on. It's one of the reasons I decided to write this book. Every week I still receive fan mail, and requests for autographs, from all over the world for the small parts I played in it. Goodness knows what Harrison Ford's mailbox is like! But I hope this book will give the lovely people who write to me more of an insight into my career before, during and after this amazing film.

It was my old mate Peter Diamond who asked me if I wanted to go to the States to work on *Return of the Jedi*. Peter was the main stunt arranger for filming in England, while Glen Randall was the stunt coordinator in the States. Not that we were allowed to call it that. Or talk about it. The security for the film was off the scale.

With Mark Hamill and a wonderful stunt crew. From left to right: Tracey Eddon, Alf Joint, Me, Mark Hamill, Peter Diamond, Paul Weston, Colin Skeaping and Dickey Beer

Any correspondence – about accommodation and schedules, for instance – referred to the production as *Blue Harvest: Horror Beyond Imagination*, or *Blue Harvest* for short. It was strongly suggested that we do the same. If we had to talk to anyone about the purpose of our visit to Arizona – Customs officers, for instance – then this was our cover. We even had to tell people we were 'specialist actors', rather than stunt performers. It really was like being in a movie – an espionage thriller!

Aside from trying to keep prying journalists off the scent for as long as possible, I've heard it said that another reason for the subterfuge was purely economic. If production facilities knew that they were negotiating with the team responsible for *Star Wars*, they'd double the price. If they thought it was a no-hope low-budget horror film, they'd be more reasonable. Of course, this tactic worked until Harrison Ford and Carrie Fisher strolled into view.

I was booked for five or six weeks' work. My parts were to include a skiff guard on Tatooine, and a storm trooper in various scenes – including fighting against the Ewoks.

I often didn't know what role I'd be doing the next day, though, such was the secrecy surrounding the production.

When I arrived in Arizona as instructed, I met up with the cast and crew at The Stardust Motor Resort Inn, in Yuma. It was certainly not the Beverly Hilton, but the atmosphere was great and it had a heart-shaped pool out the front which was well used during our stay there. We were in the desert, and it was very, very hot – sometimes the temperature hit 120 degrees.

The scenes filmed in the Yuma Desert were the exterior shoots for the Tatooine planet sequences. The cast and crew had already been filming for nearly three months at Elstree studios, back in Blighty, so production was quite well advanced. Everything was still very cloak-and-dagger – no call sheets and nothing to give away the true nature of our production, but everyone had bonded and there was a great camaraderie on set, which was infectious.

(COURTESY OF LUCASFILM LTD.LLC)

As skiff guard fighting with Luke Skywalker [Mark Hamill].
Guess who won?

Yuma was where I tore my ankle ligaments – a scene I described in the prologue to this book. It was a painful injury and very frustrating as it happened quite soon after I arrived. Suddenly, rather than being in the thick of it which is where us stunt performers like to be, I was confined to barracks, as it were. If I had to rest and recuperate, though, as I was forced to do for nearly three weeks, then there were worse places than on location with the latest *Star Wars* movie.

We were working six days a week with one day off, for good behaviour. Marion and Franklin had come with me. Franklin mainly remembers playing with Mark Hamill's son in the swimming pool, and the big stacks of Coca-Cola which were freely available. Not something you'd find on British productions back then.

Franklin poolside with Peter Mayhew (Chewbacca) and my crutches!

There was a lot of hanging around, as is usually the case on film sets, and Marion quickly struck up a friendship with Carrie Fisher. Carrie was a lovely woman as well as a brilliant actress. She was extremely funny – quick-witted and obviously super-talented. She got on with everyone and had no side to her. Carrie was also an excellent organiser. She would round up everyone to get them to go out to eat. In Yuma, the choice was limited as there weren't many restaurants, as I recall, so we'd all go out for a pizza or a burger. She'd call out to Harrison Ford, saying all the crew was going so why didn't he join us? And he would. I really enjoyed her company, as did Marion.

Me and Carrie Fisher on one of the regular crew nights out

Most of the American stunt performers were quite religious. I was brought up a Catholic and so, while the English stuntmen would run away, I'd happily sit and talk religion with them. There was a father and his son on the American stunt crew. The three of us were at lunch in Yuma one day and I had the father trying to convert me to Mormonism on one side, while his son was trying to persuade me to be a born-again Christian. I had many interesting conversations with Bob Yerkes, who was the stunt performer doubling for the Boba Fett character.

With Bob Yerkes (Boba Fett) in the Redwoods

I just couldn't imagine a similar scenario at a film set in Britain – definitely one to file under 'only in the States' – but they were all lovely people.

We tried to fit in as much as possible on our days off, especially in that period when I was incapacitated. Marion also suffered an injury. She fell over in the shower. One of the actors kindly took to rolling joints for her – to ease the pain – not something that's available on the NHS, though I believe it's legal in California now. All joking aside, it really helped her.

America was still new to me and I wanted to see as much of it as I could. This didn't always turn out as I expected. For instance, one day Marion was sitting poolside and she got chatting to a couple who were working on the film. It turned out that the man was a crop duster and had his own plane. He also did flying tours of the Grand Canyon. On hearing that, Marion was determined that we would go, but we had to get six people together to make it viable. I had just had my accident so I was on crutches but there was no way I was going to miss out. Paul Weston was also in – he was on crutches, too! We roped in Kenny Baker, the dwarf actor who played the robot R2-D2. The pilot had asked Marion if she could persuade Tracey Eddon – who was Carrie Fisher's stunt double – to make up the six, as he had a bit of a crush on her. He said he would make it a cheaper flight if she came. Marion asked her, but she had been invited to go on a boat trip that weekend. My wife said, 'Come on, you don't want to go on a boat trip when you could be with us, flying around the Grand Canyon!' so she persuaded Tracey to alter her plans.

So there we were, six of us. Me and Paul – big fellas – in the middle, Kenny and Marion in the back and Tracey upfront with the pilot in this tiny crop dusting plane. To say it was a squeeze would be an understatement. As anyone who has done it will tell you, flying above the Canyon can be a turbulent business, and our trip was like the big dipper. We were tilting up and down and bouncing around up there. The pilot had given Tracey a sick bag, and she was hyperventilating into it. She actually passed out. Tracey's one of the bravest stunt performers I know! My wife was feeling ill and the rest of us were shaken about like dry Martini, to say the least. Only Kenny seemed unaffected by it all. We must have made quite a spectacle disembarking from the plane, with Tracey and Marion feeling nauseous, and the two of us on crutches. Paul later described it as 'the ride from Hell', and this is another proper stunt performer talking!

Marion went to collect the money afterwards and Tracey paid, saying, 'But I didn't see anything!' She had been too busy

(COURTESY OF LUCASFILM LTD.LLC)

A prisoner on Endor: behind Harrison Ford and next to Carrie Fisher

concentrating on the paper bag. The boat trip would definitely have been a better option as it turned out.

After two weeks the whole production moved to the beautiful Redwood forests in Northern California. It was quite strange moving from an exposed location, where all you could see was the deep blue sky and the desert sands, to a place where we were dwarfed by the giant trees and sheltered under their canopies. There were no sandstorms interrupting filming either, like there were occasionally in Yuma. The Redwood forest is where the shots of Endor – the Ewoks' home planet – were filmed. I was recovering well and back in the action. I was working with some brilliant American stunt performers like Larry Holt and Bob Yerkes on these scenes. It was great to work with these guys – we all got along famously.

I did some scenes in the Redwood forest with Dickey Beer. One day I was a storm trooper protecting the base from the diminutive Ewoks.

One of the American stunt performers had invented a swing contraption. A dwarf actor stood on it and someone pushed them, propelling the actor in my direction, and then they would jump off the swing straight at me. It was brilliant because it really made it look like they were having a go.

It was at the end of the fortnight in the Redwood forests that I got my big break! Well, it was the piece of luck which has led to me receiving fan mail from all over the world ever since.

With Bob Yerkes, Larry Holt and an Ewok

With storm troopers Dickey Beer and Larry Holt

Peter Diamond had another film to go to, and so wanted either me or Colin Skeaping to take over from him as stunt arranger for the remaining work, which was to be done at Industrial Light & Magic's studios just north of San Francisco, in San Rafael. We tossed a coin to decide who was going to get the arranger's role. The loser would get the compensatory role of 'Biker Scout' – that's how we saw it. I called 'Tails' and then watched crestfallen as the coin span in the air and landed slowly on 'Heads'. Colin had won.

When we got to San Rafael George Lucas called us both in.

'Look,' he said, 'we don't need both of you here. You're down to play the biker scout, right, Frank?'

I nodded.

'In that case you can do your own arranging. So we don't really need you here, Colin, you can go.' I was sorry for Colin but really pleased for myself. From landing what seemed like the lesser of two positions, I was the one who was going to get an extra five days working with the delightful Carrie Fisher and Mark Hamill, while poor Colin was heading back to the UK.

(COURTESY OF LUCASFILM LTD.LLC)

Still a prisoner on Endor – with Harrison Ford

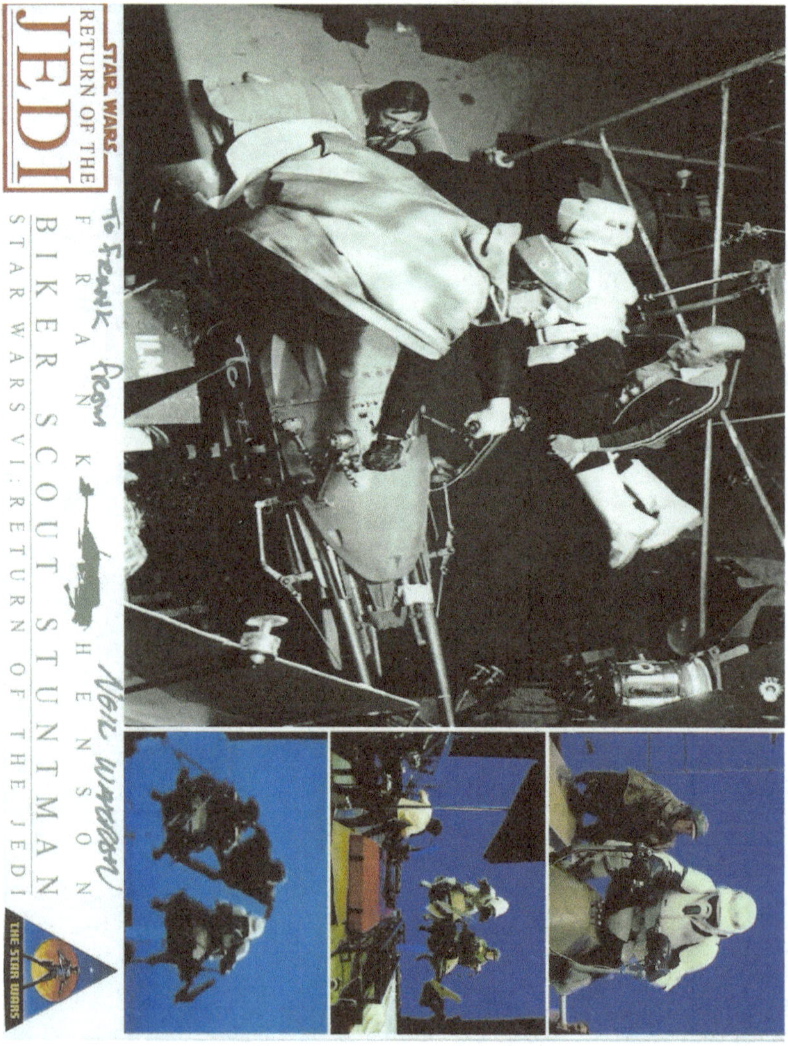

(COURTESY OF LUCASFILM LTD.LLC)

Me as Biker Scout

As I've said, it only really became apparent much later that I'd won as soon as I'd lost the toss. The speeder chase sequence became a real favourite with fans of the whole franchise. We were filming blue screen sequences which would be matched with the special Steadicam unit footage which was filmed in the Redwoods. Blue screen was cutting-edge special effects back in those days. It's far too complicated for me to get my head around but, from what Franklin tells me, it was a nightmare to get it to work properly in the early days, requiring a lot of painstaking work. Apparently green screen technology, which superseded it, is much easier. In either case the basic idea – in case you don't know – is that the actors are filmed doing a scene in the studio which is then superimposed on film footage of a different location – the Redwood forest in this instance. It was difficult to get it right using quite a static setting in those days, so it shows what an amazing director George Lucas was that he could so convincingly create the illusion of me and Mark and Carrie speeding through the air through the thick Redwood trees in the forest. The first time I saw it in the cinema I was swerving with the rest of the audience to avoid hitting the tree trunks!

It was a privilege to work with George Lucas on this sequence, even if he did get a bit frustrated with my acting skills from time to time. We had to imagine we were in the Redwood forest but all I could see was the cameras in the room – even the blue screen was behind me.

'Frank! Remember you're meant to be moving at 200 mph through the trees!' he kept reminding me. I could tell he had the whole scene playing in his head – he could see the wood for the trees, unlike me. We got there in the end.

It was also a privilege to spend more time working with Carrie Fisher. Funny, sharp, generous and wise – she really was one in a million. When we eventually had to say goodbye she signed a publicity shot for me with the words: 'Frank, if you jump into that Sarlacc pit without an adjustment [bonus] one more time you'll have

At the studio with speed bike

to buy a lot more real estate (in Yuma). Congratulations on escaping from crescent city. With love, Carrie (your night nurse).' She also signed another one to Marion and me, pretending it was from the American stunt coordinator: 'For Marion and Frank. The check's in the mail, love Glen Randall.' What a woman.

Treasured possession. A personal message from Carrie Fisher

Here's a funny story. Several years ago now there was this guy who had worked on *Return of the Jedi*. He was letting it be known that he played the biker scout. I had no way of proving it, and I began to doubt my own memory – not for the first or the last time, I can tell you. Luckily one of the wardrobe ladies had taken a photo of me in the biker scout uniform and asked if I would like one. I'd forgotten all about it until I found it while chatting to someone who was directing a film about the making of *Star Wars*. I could prove it was me and that put that argument to sleep.

I have the wardrobe lady to thank for another American 'first', which occurred while I was staying in San Francisco. One cold day – the temperature could drop in an instant on the bay – she invited us and the camera crew back to a party at her house. Her English husband saw I was cold and said,

'Do you want to get in the tub?' I had no idea what he was talking about.

'What do you mean?' I asked, wondering if this was some strange Californian ritual that I was about to be introduced to.

'It's outside,' he said, pointing into their garden.

'You're joking, aren't you? Look at that storm,' I said. Rain was lashing against the windows and I could hear the rumble of thunder above the din of the party.

'No, no, this is perfect weather for it,' he insisted. Anyway he persuaded me to get in the hot tub and it was a revelation. The steamy water bubbled away and I felt like I was back in the desert after a few minutes. It warmed me through from head to toe. He even had some plastic ducks in there which belonged to his kids. Meanwhile, the storm raged above us and San Francisco lights twinkled all around.

'I'd have got in hours ago if I'd known it was like this,' I said.

One other fond memory from working on *Return of the Jedi*. I met up again with Dave Prowse who, of course, played Darth Vader. We'd first worked together on the well-remembered British Green Cross Code public information film, from 1975. Dave played the

Green Cross Code Man, instructing children to look both ways before crossing near traffic. I drove the Austin Allegro which nearly runs over two children who hadn't been 'looking and listening all the way across the road', as he instructed. That'll teach 'em! I don't think it would be filmed like that now. Dave was a gentle giant of a man. It's often the way that the biggest villains on film are the nicest people in real life.

(COURTESY OF LUCASFILM LTD.LLC)

Another treasured possession! A personal message from Robert Watts, the British Star Wars and Indiana Jones producer and all-round lovely man. It reads: 'Frank, You must teach me to ride a Tauntaun'

While in the States we managed to cram in a bit more sightseeing. I was moved by the sight of wheelchair-bound ex-soldiers at a Veterans Day Parade. All these men who had given their all to America's wars and been rewarded with such uncertain futures. Funnily enough I'm quite anti-war now, even though I'm an ex-Para, it just seems like such a nonsensical thing to get involved in. I even went on the march against the Iraq war in London in 2003, which became the biggest-ever peacetime demonstration in Britain.

Another moving experience was visiting Dallas, and the site of President Kennedy's assassination. We drove down the road where he was killed, and even got taken to the spot in the former book depository where Oswald was said to have fired the shots. It was a strange sensation to sit in the one place and then view it from the other. Another senseless waste of life as well. I remember thinking at the time that JFK was shaping up to be a great president.

So it was an eventful two months I spent on and around *Return of the Jedi*, and the film was a huge hit when it came out. Since then, I've been invited to Star Wars conventions and been interviewed about the small parts I played in the film for various internet and fan forums. It is amazing how much interest there still is in the whole franchise, and I'm thankful that there is. At the end of the day it's a tribute to the imagination and skill of George Lucas and his team – that they managed to create this universe which doesn't look like ours, but in which people behave in pretty much the same way. I'm so proud to have contributed to it in my small way.

Stormtrooper unmasked

BOOZE AND DRUGS

I've always been someone who can 'Just say no', as the saying used to go. On many film sets, drugs were freely available, and I watched lots of people doing them, but I always walked away when I was offered something. I couldn't put anything up my nose for a start. I think I'd just sneeze. I never smoked. A lot of my old pals have died from smoking-related diseases. It's clearly a hard habit to drop. I remember asking John Wayne, who had given up smoking by the time he came over to film Brannigan,

'Duke, do you ever still fancy a cigarette?'

'Every minute of the day, kid,' was his heartfelt reply.

Drinking – I like a pint or two for Sunday lunch but, apart from then, I hardly touch the stuff. Never have. Back in the seventies, though, actors would think nothing of drinking, even while they waited to go on set.

Robert Mitchum could drink all day long – just little sips of Scotch every now and again. He asked after a mutual acquaintance in the stunt business one day, while we were sitting in his trailer. I told him,

'He's got a bit of a drinking problem at the moment,' which was, if anything, an understatement at the time.

'Has he, has he really?' said Bob with a sly glance, tipping back another Scotch.

I guess I'm just lucky in that neither booze nor drugs have ever really appealed. And the older you get, the more you see the damage they do to those around you, and you're thankful that you never took them up. Just Say No!

PETER DIAMOND

Peter Diamond was a very fine stunt arranger. He was an excellent fencer and taught a lot of people how to sword-fight. Incidentally that's how he met his wife as well, I believe.

It was a great privilege to work with Peter on Return of the Jedi. The shooting schedule was not only tight, but also top secret. Some days we didn't know what we'd be doing before we turned up at the appointed hour, but Peter was so calm and on top of things, and made sure everyone was organised and briefed.

I'd arrive in the morning and he'd say, 'You're playing a skiff guard today, Frank, go and get suited.' This might mean doing a fight scene with Mark Hamill, as Luke Skywalker, so Peter would then go through the routine with me and Mark. We'd film it and then move on to the next scene. He made it all seem easy but, like all the best arrangers, he must have been incredibly well organised and disciplined to get so much done in so little time. He was also quite shy and self-effacing when it came to taking credit. Just seeing the results of his work on the big screen was enough for him. A great man and widely respected throughout the industry.

INDIANA JONES AND THE TEMPLE OF DOOM (1984)

After *Return of the Jedi* I travelled to Africa to do some driving on *Safari 3000* with Peter Brayham, and then – thanks to Vic Armstrong – I was given the opportunity to do some more travelling. This time to Sri Lanka, to work on another huge film – *Indiana Jones and the Temple of Doom*.

It could have been so different as I nearly didn't make it on the plane. I got to the departure gate and smiled at the attendant, showing her my passport. She looked at me strangely and handed the passport back. It was Marion's. I must have picked up the wrong one by mistake in my hurry to leave on time. There was a bit of a discussion and then one of the producers stepped in and showed her my permit to work on the film, so I was allowed to board the plane. That's Hollywood magic for you, but it wasn't the only close shave I would experience on this film.

From Colombo Airport we were driven to Kandy, in the middle of Sri Lanka. As the car bounced along the uneven roads I looked out over the lush tropical vegetation and thought, not for the first time, not bad for a boy from Whitehawk.

Learning to ride an elephant in Kandy

We settled into our hotel and met up with the cast and crew already there. It was great to see Harrison Ford again, as well as many of my stunt colleagues including Vic Armstrong, who was starting to make a real name for himself, and indeed for the whole stunt profession. I'd worked on films with Vic before, but never as closely as on this one.

Vic was a true professional who took his work very seriously and had a real film-maker's eye for what would work and what wouldn't work. As a consequence, he became highly valued by many of the top directors, including Spielberg and Lucas. He was a pleasure to work with and you always felt safe with Vic because he did the prep and looked after the crew. We still get on very well

CREDIT: VIC ARMSTRONG

With Vic Armstrong on the scary rope bridge

together. He is a top-class gentleman and I was so pleased when he received recognition for his contribution to the industry – the Michael Balcon Award for Outstanding British Contribution to Cinema – at the 2002 BAFTAS.

The year before that BAFTA award, Vic received an Academy Award for Technical Achievement. And that achievement was getting one of its first outings in *Temple of Doom*. The fan descender, which Vic adapted for use in the film business, was a clever piece of equipment. It was originally used by the RAF to simulate parachute jumps inside hangars, without the need to take a plane up. It's basically a device using cables which allows a managed descent from a height. Vic had first used it to great effect in a film called *Green Ice*, where it helped him drop nearly 340 feet without injury.

It came in handy here, too.

I was down to do various small parts but my main job was doubling and standing in for Amrish Puri, the actor who was

CREDIT: VIC ARMSTRONG

With the great Amrish Puri, who I doubled, and the lovely Felix Silla, who was doubling Jonathan Ke Quan's 'Short Round' character

playing Mola Ram – the villainous leader of the Thuggee cult who has brainwashed the Maharajah.

Terry Forrestal was meant to double Amrish but he convinced Vic to use me instead of him. Terry had another film coming up and didn't want to shave his head, which was a requirement to double Amrish in this film.

Poolside with Terry Forrestal in Kandy

Vic told me he would pay me £1000 for doing this, and I replied,

'For that kind of cash you can shave my head every month.' Vic and the American stunt arranger were happy with me but, for some reason, I didn't think Spielberg was. Possibly he thought I looked too old. These things happen on movies. You just have to shrug and get on with it.

A lot of the time I was required to stand in for Amrish, while the camera operators and lighting people set up for a shot. But I also had to play him in the movie's climactic sequence.

This is where Indiana Jones and Mola Ram battle it out on a rope bridge, some 200 feet above a fast-flowing, crocodile-infested river. It was the biggest stunt sequence of the movie, and they'd built a proper bridge across a ravine.

Vic was doubling Indiana Jones. In the film, Indy cuts the bridge in half, thus disposing of a number of Mola Ram's men before doing battle with Ram himself on the cliff face, hanging onto the remnants of the bridge. In real life, the bridge was blown in places to mimic the cutting, and dummies were placed strategically on the bridge – it would have been far too dangerous for stunt performers.

CREDIT: VIC ARMSTRONG

The rope bridge breaks – I took this one under instructions from Vic!

For the combat sequences, Vic and I used his fan descenders to drop down the cliff face, from 120 feet up, then fight each other, before dropping down again. This was dangerous but the devices gave us both peace of mind, and we had a pile of boxes stacked beneath us in case we fell off. I hooked my safety belt too low for one of the takes. This caused me to spin over and Vic looked genuinely worried when he grabbed me to start pummelling me.

'I thought you'd broken away,' he grunted as we fought above the crew. The sequence looked brilliant when it was finished.

I used a fan descender again, on another sequence where Terry Forrestal and I were dropping into a river. It worked like a dream.

CREDIT: VIC ARMSTRONG

Signed by Vic – our fight on the broken rope bridge

For the close-ups of the same sequence, Harrison requested that I do a fight scene with him because Amrish wasn't so experienced in that kind of stunt fighting. This was at a mere 30 feet – still far enough up to finish you off if you don't pay attention.

I also got to film the famous scenes set in the coal mines – chasing Harrison as Indy through the labyrinth of shafts in the mining trucks.

As a 'thug' in the mine cart chase scene

All in all *The Temple of Doom* was a great film to work on – and it certainly made it worthwhile shaving my head! Thanks, Vic.

CREDIT: VIC ARMSTRONG

Harrison Ford, stunt performer Bronco McLoughlin, Wendy Leech (Vic's wife who doubled Kate Capshaw) and yours truly

SOME KIND WORDS FROM VIC ARMSTRONG

'Frank has been a pal of mine since way back when! We have had some great times together and lots and lots of laughs. I have affectionately always nicknamed Frank "Lead Boot", because if Frank was going to do a crash for you he never left anything behind, he really was fearless. Well, fearless unless I put him in an acting part which he hated doing, so of course I would make sure I always gave Frank an acting part and if possible an acting part with lines!

On Temple of Doom I gave him the key part of one of Mola Ram's cohorts. He had to pop up over a ledge and frighten Kate Capshaw to death. We had great fun rehearsing him and deliberately giving him the wrong cues! We were mean bunch really but we only did it because we loved Frank so much. On the day when Spielberg was there, and I gave Frank the right cue, he did it perfectly of course, and we celebrated that night with a few beers.

I think I will call Frank and tell him I have a nice part for him in my next show, with only two pages of dialogue, just to hear the silence on the other end of the phone for a few seconds. Frank is a great stuntman and a great friend and I owe a lot to him for all the great work he has done for me.'

OCTOPUSSY (1983)

From one action hero to another. I was onto my third Bond now – Roger Moore. Clowns feature throughout *Octopussy*, right from the opening sequence where a British agent – 009 – is being pursued, dressed as a clown, by two assassins. I appear in the circus sequence as one of many clowns who create chaos while Bond is trying to defuse a nuclear bomb. This sequence was also notable for the character Francisco the Fearless, the human cannon ball, who was played by none other than my old mate Dickie Graydon. You can tell he was having a whale of a time. Dickie loved being shot out of that cannon. He must have done it about 25 times.

Aside from the clowning around, this film once again brought home to me the bravery of many of my fellow stunt performers, and the very real danger we put ourselves through in the name of our craft. It's certainly not all clowning around.

My dear friend Martin Grace had been Roger Moore's stunt double since *The Spy Who Loved Me* (1977). Martin and I first worked together on *You Only Live Twice,* in the famous volcano scenes I described earlier.

In *Octopussy*, he had a difficult sequence to prepare for where he doubles James Bond, making his way along a moving train as it heads towards a tunnel. The stunt took place on the Nene Valley steam railway, in the British Midlands. For some reason, the production team had missed a concrete wall which ran parallel to part of the railway track. As Martin bravely climbed along the outside of the carriages, looking in, he ran full pelt into the wall, breaking his pelvis and damaging his thigh. As he looked down he could actually see the thigh bone through a wound in his leg. Nevertheless, he clung onto the train until it could be stopped. He was hospitalised for months which was bad enough, but it could have been worse. Needless to say, as soon as Martin had recovered, he was back performing.

NEVER SAY NEVER AGAIN (1983)

You wait for one Bond and then two come along at once. My next film marked the controversial return of Sean Connery to the role of 007. It was controversial because the film was made outside of the official Eon Productions organisation, run by the Broccoli family.

Sean was 52, which sounds quite young now (even Daniel Craig is over 50), but at the time was considered ancient for Bond. He portrayed Bond as an aging secret agent being brought back into the field for one last mission. It was also Connery's last appearance in the role, and I thought he was terrific.

This was one of my favourite working experiences. Vic Armstrong was the stunt coordinator and we had become good friends by then. He rang me and asked if I wanted to come on-board and spend three weeks down in the South of France driving and horse riding. It's a hard life, this stunt malarkey.

The three weeks soon became six, due to an unfortunate accident. Roy Alon, one of the stunt performers, rolled a car over the wrong way and wrote it off. While we were waiting for a replacement car, Vic decided to film a sequence where Bond on horseback is being chased through a castle by Arab villains, also on horseback. At one point they cross this narrow bridge and Bond, doubled by Vic, was meant to surge between two of the baddies, pushing them and their horses to the left and the right of him. Vic dislocated his ankle when his stirrup got caught on one of the horses. That was bad enough, but one of the other riders – a Spanish stuntman – landed on a wall and broke his back.

Vic asked me to stand in for the Spanish lad and it was then decided that the riding sequences should be completed before the car rolling was refilmed, so that was another three weeks for me. The Spanish riders were brilliant – I learned a lot just watching the way they handled their horses and taught them to do tricks. They were some of the best riders I've ever seen, and it was a pleasure to work with them.

The horse I was given to work with was the only one they had available and he was what they call a 'falling horse'. This just meant that he had been trained to fall down on cue. He wasn't a horse usually used for the standard riding sequences. The Spanish guy who handed him to me said,

'You know how to ride this horse? Don't push it too hard because he'll fall down. Don't pull too hard on the reins because he'll think that's the cue and down he'll go.' This is the last thing we needed now that the schedule had been delayed by accidents and mishaps.

I said,

Me with some of the Spanish riders, and Roy Alon, *Never Say Never Again*

'Don't you worry – he'll hardly realise I'm on his back.' We got on just fine and I had an extra three weeks in the southern sun with my new Spanish friends. Bliss. The horse riding sequence we were filming climaxed with Vic taking a spectacular 40-foot fall on a horse over the castle battlements. But that was shot on a later date and at a different location – the magic of film!

We then returned to the car-rolling sequence. In these scenes I ended up swapping gender again to double for Barbara Carrera, who was playing a Russian agent sent to kill Bond. Bond comes home to find another agent dead and hears footsteps running down the stairs. The Russian assassin (me) gets into a Renault 5 Turbo and speeds off. Bond jumps onto a motorbike and gives chase. Vic had got me in to do the driving for Barbara while American biker Mike Runyard was doubling Sean Connery on the motorcycle. We had a few great stunts in that sequence: one where Roy Alon had to turn over the car, while I swept through the shot in the Renault. The timing had to be spot on and it was. The second was a big bike jump over the docks.

It's well worth a look if you haven't seen it, or maybe that's just my professional pride talking. The stunts were tricky but everyone was at the top of their game and they looked great when the film came out, to widespread critical acclaim. I was proud to be a part of this movie. And I never say never to working in the South of France.

THE LAST DAYS OF POMPEII (1984)

This was Franklin's first venture into the world of movie work. He was only 15 when he was working on it. But I need to digress a bit.

When Franklin was 13 it was time for him to leave Hill House School – which he loved – we hunted high and low for a good school to get him into. Because I was working abroad a lot, and Marion often accompanied me, we thought it would be a good idea to get him into a boarding school if possible. We tried several places, including Bedales, Rugby and Hurst College, but nowhere was quite the right fit. Someone at Hurst suggested Millfield. Franklin had been diagnosed with dyslexia, and they had what used to be called a remedial section there. At the time, it was the most expensive school in the country, but fortunately I was making a lot of money by then.

Once again, I was hauled into the headmaster's office. After a long conversation, with me sitting on the edge of my seat, he coughed and looked embarrassed.

'I have to ask you honestly, Mr Henson,' he said. 'Can you afford the fees?'

'If I couldn't, I wouldn't be here,' I replied, relaxing back into the chair. That was that. He was in. The first night, Franklin later told us, he cried. He wasn't used to being away from home. But after that he settled right in and had a great time. He's that way. Makes friends easily – everybody likes him.

At the age of 14, Franklin joined the Film Artistes' Association. I told them that Franklin was actually 16 because he was already tall. He did extras work in the school holidays. Just like his dad, he had the work ethic from an early age. Peter Diamond got him his first big job on *The Last Days of Pompeii* (1984) TV series when he was 15. Franklin played an Egyptian soldier.

This was when the unions still had some clout, so he automatically earned extra money for anything considered additional to the usual extra requirements. Wearing a skirt and make-up above the knees? Extra money. A crocodile papier mâché head? Impaired vision – extra money. Carrying an actor on a litter throne? Unreasonable weight load – extra money. It came to the end of the day and he ran down with his chit, queued up and waited to get paid in cash. He was counting it up – £150! For a teenager in 1984, that was a lot of money. He put his thumb over it. They asked,

'Can you come back tomorrow?'

'Yesss!' he said. And he was off. The next day he couldn't get there quickly enough. If I couldn't take him onto sets then one of my pals usually could, so he got to know quite a few people in the business while he was still very young. And that was him set until he got onto the stunt register when he was 19 years old.

THE AMBASSADOR (1984)

I was reunited with my first-ever director, J. Lee Thompson, in Israel on *The Ambassador* – a film about an American ambassador who tries to bring peace to the Middle East through his own initiatives. This film starred two of my favourite actors, Robert Mitchum and Rock Hudson. Dorothy Ford was there as the main female stunt performer.

I have two main memories from this experience. The first was sitting in the car with Hudson for a car chase sequence. Now Lee had told me previously what was going to happen, but told me not to tell Rock, as he thought this might produce a bigger reaction. He wasn't wrong.

'Action!' called the director and we set off. As we're driving at high speed, a car appeared from the side out of nowhere, driven by Dorothy, and I had to manoeuvre sharply to escape it. Hudson nearly jumped out of his seat. We had to shoot it again. Rock was furious that he had not been warned.

'Why the hell didn't anyone tell me?' he complained.

'Sorry, Rock,' I replied. 'Lee told me not to tell you.'

'If I had known, I would have been ready for it!' Hudson said angrily.

With Rock Hudson, filming *The Ambassador*

I got talking to Robert Mitchum about Ireland, a place we both loved. He told me he'd been working on a film somewhere in the South.

'I was in a pub, and I got punched by a big man. Blood and snot went everywhere!'

A bit later, I was speaking with his long-time stunt double, and I asked why Mitchum had got punched. He said that Robert was sitting in the bar and a young woman came up to him and asked for his autograph.

Robert said, 'Yeah, sure,' and wrote, 'I would like to f*** you, Robert Mitchum.' The lady was upset and so she had gone and told her boyfriend, and he had gone back and asked Robert to stand up, then smacked him one on the nose. Everyone in the pub had started to fight.

I replied, 'Yeah, that sounds like an Irish pub!'

The stunt double and I had another encounter which was quite amusing. We were filming a fight sequence and 'thwack!' he hit me for real.

'God, I'm so sorry, Frank,' he said, 'that's the first time I've done that in twenty years.' So we went again and he hit me again! I said,

'Don't tell me, that's the second time in twenty years – and both times me!' We became great mates after that.

Signed photo from Robert Mitchum. It reads, 'Frank, next time let's make it somewhere in the Caribbean. Cheers. Robert Mitchum'

GOING UNDERCOVER (ORIGINALLY KNOWN AS YELLOW PAGES (1984))

This was a big turning point in my career, even if the movie sank without trace on its release, as I almost did during the filming in Denmark. It's a film about a maverick tour guide who ends up getting chased by the FBI. It was meant to be a vehicle for Jack Lemmon's son, Chris, to make his name in but the reviews were awful. *The Hollywood Reporter* even apologised for their review the week after saying words to the effect of – *it wasn't actually that bad* – but it was. As a mate of mine said, *you can't put sequins on a turd.*

Jim Dowdall had asked me if I'd do the car stunts on it, because he knew I had the bottle. Jim and I went way back. He'd handed Richard Burton the pistol he shot me with on *Where Eagles Dare*. The main stunt, which nearly cost me my life, was basically this. A car goes out of control, crashes through a shed, taking half the shed wall with it, goes up a couple of small ramps and ends up in the harbour.

The car had been prepared to float in the water. Jim and the stunt team had rigged up a pulley system to get the car up to 50 miles per hour as it went through the balsa woodshed. Ironically, there was no driving for me to do. The engine had been removed and there wasn't even any steering as the car was being pulled along the pulley lines. There was a 'quick-release' mechanism for the pulley at the top of the ramp, so all I had to do was sit in the car and pretend to drive. It should have been the simplest car stunt ever for me.

At this point in the story the car had lost its roof, after being driven under an articulated lorry, so it was now effectively a convertible. The two 'A' posts – which hold the windscreen in place – were still there but the windscreen had gone. Jim wanted me to have some protection as I went through the shed, so he had fitted a Makrolon shield – which is shatterproof perspex – and he told me to stay below the windscreen line as I went through the shed.

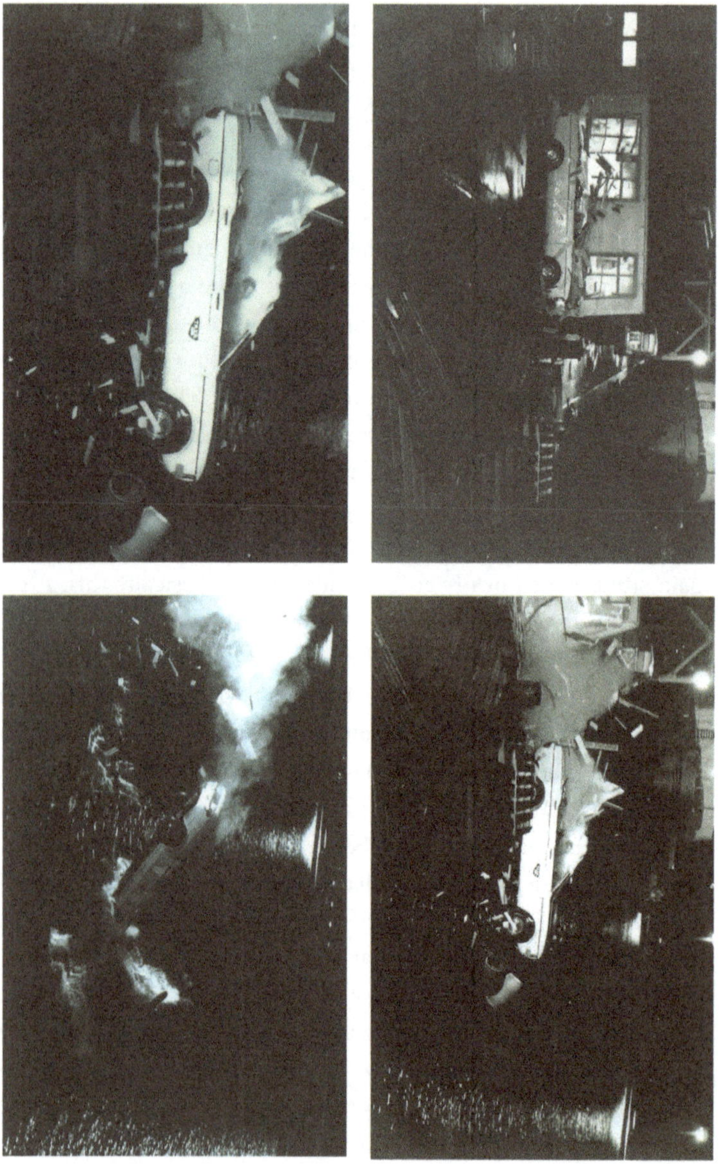

PHOTOS: ROLF KONOW

My accident on *Yellow Pages*. Going through the shed and into the harbour. By the second photo I was unconscious

Gareth Milne was sitting in the back of the car.

'This is fucking dangerous,' he said to me.

'I'm only getting £750,' I said. 'Still, getting a grand for the next shot – jumping a bridge. Should be a piece of cake after this.' He laughed nervously. I knew it was a dangerous stunt – I'm not stupid when it comes to my safety, or the safety of people I'm working with. But I thought, well I'm here now, and it's what I do for a living. I don't want to let them down and, at the end of the day, it's a job. My one fear was that, if the car turned over in the harbour, it was 2am, a cold night, and the divers might not be able to find me in time.

I was wearing a harness for the impact with the water. Jim said,

'As you approach the hut, squat down – just roll sideways slightly until you've gone through. Then, as you feel the car lifting off the ramps, you can sit up again and brace yourself for impact with the water.' As Jim tells it, I ducked down as planned just before hitting the hut, but I must have sat up again before the car had crashed through. I remember nothing of this. A whole three-inch plank of balsa hit the left side of my head and cut my head open from front to back. To make things worse, there was a net curtain attached to the plank with staples, so they had gone under the skin as well. So there was a flap of skin and a lot of blood – head injuries always bleed profusely. It was just very unfortunate – I had probably sat up just two yards too soon. Thankfully I was unconscious for most of this. Gareth was still in the back of the car but he'd managed to avoid the impact, so he and the rescue boat got me out of the harbour and dragged me into an ambulance, off to hospital.

Jim told me he'd got on the phone to Marion to tell her. Typically she was no nonsense.

'What's the silly bastard done now?' was her response which was great. She said she was going to get a plane out the next day, and then she phoned Franklin's school to let him know what had happened and that I was going to be alright.

Jim came back to the hospital and sat with Gareth as I started to come to. He asked me where I was. I'd just finished *Wild Geese II* in Germany, with Laurence Olivier and Lewis Collins, which is why I must have said,

'I'm in Germany, aren't I?' and he said,

'No.'

'Holland?' I guessed.

'No, you're in Denmark,' and then I remembered,

'Oh yeah, yeah, Denmark – *Yellow Pages*.'

'Are you married?'

'Yes.'

'Have you got any children?'

'I've got one son.'

With each correct answer I could see him looking more and more relieved.

'Tell me about your new house,' he said.

'What new house?'

'The one you won't stop talking about. In St Peter's Square.' I'd just bought this beautiful four-storey house in a prestigious London square but I couldn't remember the first thing about it. Later, the brain surgeon who had operated on me explained that, in the accident, I'd lost my immediate short-term memory, but longer-term memories were relatively unaffected. That's why I could remember my marriage and my son, but not the house.

I said, 'Tell this man to stop stitching me up.'

'I'm putting you back together,' the doctor said. I didn't realise what a state I was in at that stage. He apologised for not being able to administer any pain relief because there wasn't enough solid skin to inject it into. The truth was I couldn't feel any pain, there was probably still a ton of adrenalin coursing round my system.

'Thank God your skull's not broken,' the doctor said.

Jim asked me,

'Do you remember anything that happened?'

'No, I remember going towards the shed and that's about it really.' I was in a cast and laid up in bed but I made a remarkable recovery – I was only there for one day. They'd put stitches in and wanted to keep me in for observation but thankfully Marion took me back to England – I don't like to linger in hospitals. Jim said to Marion,

'Frank's as hard as bloody nails,' which pleased me no end.

I'd been injured before, of course – torn ligaments, cuts and bruises. It goes with the territory. But I'd never experienced anything like this. It even made the newspapers, which is more than could be said for the film.

'We're not getting paid enough for this,' said Jim.

'I know,' I said.

The element of danger is always there in this job. People pay us to do the things which aren't considered safe for the actors to do. No one wants to get hurt, and all the best possible safety measures are put in place to prevent it happening but at the end of the day there is always a chance you'll end up getting hurt. But you can't really call yourself a

Me and my stitches. Shortly after the accident on *Yellow Pages*

stunt performer unless you're prepared to take these risks. I've never done 100 feet falls, though I've done 40 feet. But cars were a speciality of mine, and I took pride in being able to meet any challenge.

I had 74 stitches in my head. The scars are still visible to this day. People often ask if I was insured while doing these stunts. The answer is yes, but not for a lot of money. Not really, when you consider what's at stake. You might get £50,000 if the job kills you. I've never made a claim. Maybe things have changed. I hope so.

KING SOLOMON'S MINES (1985)

I was back with J. Lee Thompson again the following year. I had just finished working on *Top Secret! a* comedy by the *Airplane* team, where I played a German officer who gets kicked in the face. It was only a week's work.

Around this time, Peter Diamond called and asked me to come and work for him on *King Solomon's Mines* – as a German officer! It was a part I played a lot in those days. There were a lot more war films back then, and when your face gets noted for something it sticks.

The production was filmed in Zimbabwe, and starred Richard Chamberlain and Sharon Stone. It was a gentle parody of the Indiana Jones movies: you can tell this from the film posters alone, which used the same style of lettering. One of my stunts involved me chasing after Richard and yelling to him in German.

J. Lee Thompson asked me if I spoke any German.

'German?' I replied. 'I have trouble speaking bloody English!'

Thankfully he laughed and said,

'Don't worry, Frank, we'll dub you instead.'

Thank God for that! I thought, otherwise on top of everything else I would have had some awkward lines to learn. The sequence I most remember was tough enough as it was. I'm running through the carriages after Richard, yelling German so to speak, and he climbs down under the train to try and get away, then I'm climbing down after him. He's got nowhere to go and we have a fight – kicks and punches are thrown – but then Richard grabs a steam line from under the train and pulls the hose on me. I fall off the train and, back in real life, I roll down the embankment to safety. It was a really good sequence and as we managed it in one take with a small cut.

Peter Diamond really earned his money, and justified his reputation, with a moment of genius on this production. There was a day when we couldn't get permission from the authorities to move the train. Lee tasked Peter to find a way around the problem. As always, the schedule was very tight.

'How can we make it look like the train is moving?' Lee asked him.

With Richard Chamberlain and one of the African stunt boys on *King Solomon's Mines*

Peter said,

'Leave it to me, boss,' and gave it some thought. A while later he gathered some of the boys to cut down some branches from nearby trees. Then he explained to Lee what he had planned.

As Lee shouted,

'Action!' we ran down the back of the train holding the branches above our heads. The camera filmed the branches through the train windows. It was like that effect you get when you're sitting on a train and it leaves a platform, but it looks like the platform's moving away. When it was played back on film, it actually looked like the train was moving. Every time I see the movie on TV I just smile, as it looks so great. Peter Diamond really was a fine stuntman and one of the best stunt arrangers in the business. No wonder he was always working.

A VIEW TO A KILL (1985)

I did a few stunts on this for Martin Grace, who had thankfully made a full recovery from his terrible accident on *Octopussy*. Bob Simmons was the stunt coordinator. There's a sequence in the film where the baddie Max Zorin, played by the brilliant Christopher Walken, floods a mine he owns in an attempt to submerge Silicon Valley and gain a monopoly on the world's production of microchips. That's all well and good but the mine is still full of his loyal workers, one of whom was being played by me, and we get washed away in the force of the water through the mine shafts.

The way we showed this in the production was by using 'tip tanks'. These are massive studio tanks which hold tonnes of water which can be released to simulate effects like sudden flooding. Well, you can control where the water goes, but controlling the effect it has on the human body is another matter. I can vouch for that. These are, after all, real torrents of water, and they really take the wind out of you when they hit you. For this type of stunt

I would always cover my options for safety. Will I catch my arms? Better wear arm pads. Will I hit my knees on the mine shaft set? Best wear knee pads. Despite all this preparation, I had forgotten my back protector. As I was swept away by the force of the water, I smashed my lower back on a wall. The pain was tremendous and caused me a great deal of discomfort for about three months, but I learned from my mistake. Once bitten, they say ... and they're not wrong.

REVOLUTION (1985)

I'll be honest – my memories of *Revolution* don't have a lot to do with stunts. Al Pacino was the star of the movie – a British historical epic about the American Revolution – but for me the real star was, and will always be, a horse.

In spite of being set in America, *Revolution* was filmed in Britain in Norfolk and Devon – part of the reason it bombed at the box office, according to a few of the critics at the time. Eddie Stacey was the stunt coordinator and there was a huge team, as I recall. It was certainly an expensive movie to make. There were lots of ex-military drafted in as extras for the battle scenes, and also a lot of time was taken with training horses. Eddie bought seven or eight horses specifically for the production, but they were all ex-racehorses and they had never been coached for film. It's a specialised skill, training horses. A great mate of mine, Stevie Dent, is one of the best horse men in the business. On a film set, you need animals that don't get easily spooked by loud noises or flashes of light. If the lead actor needs to ride, then that horse might literally be carrying the film on its back. In the old days there was a lot of cruelty in the way horses were made to fall down – their hooves might be attached to the reins with wires which would then be pulled to force them to the ground. Many horses were killed during filming or destroyed soon after. As you might have realised by now, I can't abide any animal suffering.

It breaks my heart. Mercifully there are regulations in place now to stop animals being mistreated on set. Any scenes involving animals are supervised by safety officers.

Anyway, the horses on *Revolution* needed a lot of care and encouragement, so we got to know them very well. There was one horse I became very attached to. A pal of mine who was riding on the film – Bryan Bowes – told me that the horses were going to be auctioned once the movie was wrapped, and he was thinking about going along. So I said,

'If you're going, Bryan, will you bid on that one for me?' He said he would. I already had a lovely old mare, which I'd bought from Bryan for my son, Franklin, and I thought this one would make a great horse for him and I'd then have the mare. We'd be able to ride together.

He was skint at the time, poor Bryan, but he was as good as his word and he bought him for me for £600. We named the horse Serpico, after the Al Pacino crime movie. He had a bit of life in him and a bit of a dark side, like Pacino's cop. So now Franklin and I each had a horse. He took an immediate shine to Serpico and managed him really well – he could be a bit of a handful, as I was to find out. We were out one day, and Franklin said,

'Do you want a go on him, Dad?' I said,

'Yes, of course, I'd love to.'

So he's on my horse, and I'm on Serpico, and we've taken off across the downs and suddenly I realise I can't stop this horse. I'm shouting,

'Get out of the way!' and people are diving left and right to avoid me. Luckily, I knew where I was heading. I knew there was this swampy area up ahead so I pulled right towards it and we went hurtling in. Serpico pulled up and launched me over his head. Thankfully it was a soft landing. Although when I got home my wife wasn't best pleased – I was covered head-to-toe in mud.

'Where have you been?' she said, looking me up and down. Beautiful horse Serpico was, though. We had him for a few years, though I only took him out a couple of times. Franklin quickly became a much better rider than me. He had been working out in Mexico for six months and got used to the style of riding out there. He'd even brought back a western horse saddle, to try on the horses. He said to me,

'I'm going out riding this morning,' and asked if I wanted to join him. I told him unfortunately I had to head back to London, which is where we were mainly living at the time.

I'd only reached Epsom when the phone in the car rang. It was Franklin. He said,

'Dad, can you come back?' I said,

'I can't – what's the matter?' He said,

'It's Serpico. He's dead. There's been an accident.'

I was devastated.

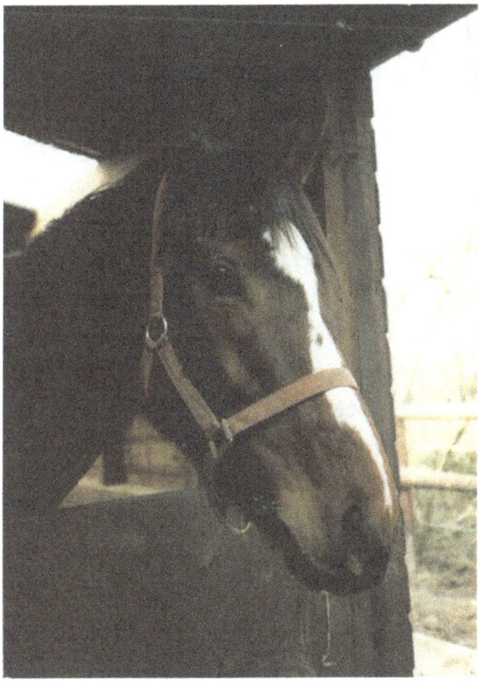

Rest in peace, Serpico

What had happened was that Serpico hadn't been out for a ride with Franklin for a long time, only with me, and so was obviously quite excited. When Franklin put the western saddle on him, it felt strange because it had a double cinch on it – which was not what he was used to. So he reared up and fell back onto a broken jockey wheel which was attached to a trailer in the corner of my front yard. He stabbed himself to death. I could cry thinking about it now. Serpico is buried in one of my fields, near where we live in West Sussex. He's what I think about anytime I see *Revolution* is on TV, or someone mentions the film to me.

EDGE OF DARKNESS (1985)

I worked with Martin Campbell on this critically acclaimed nuclear thriller TV series. It was later remade as a film which was nowhere near as well received. I was the stunt arranger – a position I didn't often hold – but I was working with Martin Campbell and we had a great working relationship, so I felt at ease. I got Terry Plummer, who I'd worked with on many films since the early *Casino Royale*, to double Joe Don Baker while I doubled the lead actor Bob Peck – who plays the grieving Detective Ronald Craven.

It was a strange job in some ways. Bob Peck wanted to do all his own stunts while Joe Don Baker didn't want to do any of his. That can be a headache – it's generally easier if the actors let you get on with what you've been paid to do. At the same time, you've got to admire them for having a go – especially when they might put themselves at risk.

There was one funny incident I remember. Terry was carrying a backpack which looked identical to the one carried by Don Baker, while he was acting as his double. Don Baker's backpack was full of props and tools that his character would need in the scene – so it was quite heavy. But Terry had taken all the stuff out of his bag and replaced it with cardboard, thinking, what's the point in lugging this lot up a hill if I don't need to? After a couple of days' filming, Don Baker picked up Terry's bag by mistake and realised there was nothing in it. To say he went absolutely potty would be an understatement.

'What the fuck is going on? Why am I carrying all this gear when he's not?' He was furious. Once Terry and the rest of us had composed ourselves, Terry gave him his proper bag back. Sometimes actors get so absorbed in their roles that they fail to see the funny side of situations like this. I think Joe did in the end, though, to be fair to him.

THE BEST STUNT I EVER DID?

CASUALTY (1987)

I believe I did one of the best stunts of my life – and one of the most difficult – on *Casualty*. Yes, that's right. Not a megabucks Hollywood production, or an all-action adventure movie, but the long-running BBC TV medical drama. I organised it, too. I was glad that Franklin was there to witness it at close hand – very close hand as it turned out. But don't worry – no one ended up in A&E. Sadly I don't have any photos of it, so I'll have to paint you a picture with words.

The story around the stunt was that some kids had locked one of their friends in the boot of a car. The car was parked on a hill and when they let off the handbrake, at 2 in the morning, the car careered down the hill, through a building into a room full of wedding party-goers.

I was manoeuvring the car, but had to remain unseen, as the only person in the car was meant to be locked in the boot. The party-goers were mainly stunt people. I used my son, Franklin, as I knew he was very gutsy, and Sarah Franzl, an incredible stunt performer, as I knew she was also very brave. These two took the main impact from the collision and the other performers, including

Peter Brayham and Dave Holland, had to scatter as they saw the car crash through the wall. Well, you would, wouldn't you?

The way I'd arranged it was this. I'd taken the driver's seat out and I was lying on the floor of the car. I had a mirror in front of me which reflected the image from a mirror on the back window, which therefore showed me a view in front of the car and allowed me to steer the vehicle where it was meant to go. So I moved down the hill, holding the bottom of the steering wheel so I was out of sight, hit a car and then we cut. Then I steered the car further down, hit another car and then we cut again.

Now we get to the big stunt. In the room full of party-goers, I'd put a railway sleeper a couple of metres in front of the camera to stop the car crashing into the camera crew. Franklin and Sarah, and the other wedding guests, were dancing away in front of this. They can't see me because I've got to crash through two sets of doors – set in a small partition wall and a breeze-block wall – to reach them. But they can hear me revving the engine outside. Franklin said to Sarah, as they were nervously shuffling from one foot to the other in time to the music,

'Fucking hell, what speed is he coming in at?'

The problem for them was this. Normally when you're being knocked down by a car as a stunt performer you can see it coming. This means you know when to jump up on the bonnet without telegraphing that this is what you're about to do. They didn't have that luxury, though, as the car was going to come smashing through a wall just a few feet away from them while they were meant to be casually dancing away like you do at a wedding party. As Franklin said to me afterwards with some understatement,

'You just have to grit your teeth and get on with it.'

I'd estimated I needed to be going at least 15 miles per hour to make it through those walls. Perhaps I ended up going a little faster. I was concerned that, if I couldn't get through the two sets of doors first time, then the impact would nevertheless bring the ceiling down, ruining the set and they wouldn't have time to rebuild it. They'd put a lot of dirt and dust up there to make the crash spectacular. The fact that it was the middle of the night didn't help as I couldn't see what was in front of me very well.

So I revved up, set off at a speed and 'bang!' went straight through the partition wall, then 'bang!' straight through the breeze-blocks. By now the extras and other stunt performers had gone, as they heard me coming, but there were Franklin and Sarah, padded up, and they jumped up onto the bonnet just in time as the roof came down and the car crashed into the sleeper. Worked first take. Peter Brayham thought I'd crushed them. There was so much dust no one could see anything. The next week they fired me because they said I'd been driving too fast. In my eyes I thought I did a great job. It's not easy controlling a car from the floor through two mirrors at the best of times. At 2am it's very tricky indeed. Oh well, no harm done. Both me and *Casualty* are still going strong, thirty years later!

THE LIVING DAYLIGHTS (1987)

I was on the lovely Rock of Gibraltar for the filming of the pre-title sequence. Paul Weston was the coordinator on this, Timothy Dalton's first Bond film. Paul had assembled a terrific crew, including Val Musetti, the lovely Dorothy Ford, Terry Forrestal and Rémy Julienne and his family. We had some great nights out. Rémy is a French stunt driving legend – a former motocross champion who has appeared in over 1400 films. He is 87 now – even older than me. It was an honour to work with him.

In the sequence, which was filmed mainly on a short stretch of road right near the top of the rock, a Russian assassin has commandeered a Land Rover, and is driving the vehicle even more recklessly than me in *Casualty*. In fact it was a member of Rémy's family hurtling down the mountainside, and very skilfully, too. My job was to play a pedestrian who had to get the hell out of the way, very quickly, which is exactly what I did. Some people think it looks easy – throwing yourself out of the path of a speeding car – and that you could get extras to do this rather than paying for stunt performers. It is not. You have to judge the timing just right. It mustn't look like you knew the vehicle was coming, like you've moved before your character would have realised they were in danger. That will spoil the shot. But you have to react quickly enough to make it look good for the camera, and to keep yourself safe of course. No, it's always better to use stunt boys and girls in the background of action scenes like this one.

On the Rock of Gibraltar for *The Living Daylights*

THE MONEY SHOT

With stunts, it's all about the money shot. This means that everything has to be larger than life – even just throwing a punch. For example, if the camera is behind the guy who gets hit, his head has to bounce backwards, not just move slightly to one side as it might in real life.

When you're turning a car over you don't want it to gently wobble onto its side. You want it to flip over and over, doors coming off and skidding until it comes to a satisfying rest some distance from where it set off. The money shot.

FULL METAL JACKET (1987)

By now, I had a reputation for being quite gutsy – for being willing to put myself on the line where perhaps a few others wouldn't really fancy it. So, I wasn't too put out when Jim Dowdall rang me up and asked,

'Do you fancy being in an exploding lorry?'

'How much?' I asked.

'A thousand?'

'All day long,' I answered.

I was also excited to be in a film directed by the legendary Stanley Kubrick, although I was a bit apprehensive as he had a reputation for being really moody.

Although the film was set in the Vietnam War, it was mainly filmed in Cambridgeshire, England, as well as Newham in East London and the Isle of Dogs. I was there with Franklin, who was training for the stunt register, and already quite experienced for his 16 years.

The time arrived for my exploding van stunt. Funny, but it was one of those French trucks they turn into pizza vans now. Well, this was the hottest pizza delivery I was ever going to make. In the film I was playing the part of a Viet Cong suicide bomber, driving an explosive-packed lorry through the barrier protecting a Marine camp before detonating his load to cause maximum damage.

My reality didn't feel that far removed, though I certainly didn't intend to kill myself or anybody else for that matter. I was sitting in the front of the van in a fireproof box. I was wearing a fire jacket and a crash helmet. There was padding all around me, to protect me from the detonation of the explosives packed in the back of the van. I also had earmuffs on under the helmet, which Franklin had fixed to the side of my head with gaffer tape, because we couldn't get them to stay in place otherwise.

IIIIIIIIIIII

In contrast to what I'd read or heard, Stanley Kubrick was very pleasant and thoughtful. We discussed the route of the van. Stanley showed me the positions of his five cameras, which would be on me as I hurtled through the checkpoint. He asked,

'Are my cameras safe?' and I said,

'Yes, sir, I'll probably blow it about here,' and I indicated the spot where I would detonate the explosives.

'And how about you?' he asked. 'Will you be alright? Will you be able to get out if the lorry rolls over? Can we get you out in time if you get stuck?' I pointed,

'I've got my son here, we've got the fire brigade over there, I don't think there'll be too much of a problem.'

'Great.'

Kubrick also had a reputation for being meticulous – he infamously reshot a scene in *The Shining* 127 times, which got him into *The Guinness Book of Records*. I was hoping that I wouldn't be repeatedly blown up in an exploding truck for the next two weeks. I didn't think my nerves were up to it.

I sat in the van, the adrenalin flooding through me. I might be 'gutsy' but it doesn't mean I don't get nervous on stunts like this – especially ones involving fire or explosives – they can be the hardest to predict in terms of damage or effect. When I heard 'Action!' I floored it, every muscle tensed for the blast, but the cab door came open as I was approaching the camp gate at speed, so I stopped the van and we reset. Now I was wired. On the second take I crashed through the barrier and hit the detonator at exactly the right place. Boom! Up in the air I went in the truck. Franklin came rushing up to help me out of the lorry cab. I was a bit shaken, smelling of petrol and cordite. The shock wave from the blast had hit me in the bollocks. When I tried to take off the helmet, the gaffer tape was singed to my head, so Franklin had to cut my hair off. I was not best pleased, I can tell you.

Jim Dowdall said to me later,

'That was a hell of a bang – a serious bang. Even Kubrick looked taken aback at the size of the explosion and the fact that you walked out of it.'

But Stanley Kubrick was happy. The take was good, thank the Lord. I had delivered the pizza.

'Thank you very much,' he said as I brushed myself down and reflected that it could easily have gone a lot worse.

THE BEAST OF WAR (1988)

Kevin Reynolds was the director of this gritty war film, about a Soviet tank that gets lost in an Afghan valley and pursued by a group of rebels. Paul Weston had assembled a great stunt team again, including Tracey Eddon and Wayne Michaels. The movie was filmed in Israel. I was a tank commander on a Soviet T-55 tank. I can honestly say that the special effects team must have had a blast, rigging up the tanks, because the sound from the tank's gun was ear-bursting.

Paul was at the top of his game, which is pretty much as good as it gets.

In fact, I'd go as far as to say that a stunt he devised and performed for this film is up there in my top three favourite stunts of all-time (see page 167). Paul plays a mujahideen fighter who is deliberately crushed to death by a Soviet tank crew as an act of revenge. He is lying in a rut and the tank slowly rolls over the length of him. In fact, Paul had built a recessed hole in the ground which he disguised with dirt, and which allowed him to withdraw

Filming on *The Beast of War* – one of the quieter moments!

safely underneath the tank as it passed over him. You can see him almost hugging the tank tracks as he is run over. It was a brilliantly effective stunt.

I have admired Paul Weston from the very first time we worked together – on *Z Cars*, the early British TV crime drama, in 1964. We got to know each other properly on *Casino Royale*, in 1966, when Paul was still an extra. Then in the seventies, on shows like *The* Sweeney, we worked together quite regularly. When Paul graduated to stunt coordinator, he employed me a lot for my driving skills in particular, but also other stunt work. He was kind enough to praise my timing. I suppose if I'm known for a skill it's my driving where – like comedy – timing is everything. Paul brought something different to every film he worked on – he has a great vision for how stunts will look on film, which is a rare gift.

Me and Franklin go into business

WILLOW (1988)

This fantasy adventure was written by George Lucas and directed by Ron Howard and had a great stunt team, including Franklin. He wasn't quite a qualified stunt performer, so he was still working as an extra, but he was already a very good horse rider. He ended up working alongside the stunt team and filling in as required. This was an advantage you get from attending an institution like Millfield – not many other pupils learn to play polo at their school. To him it was all great fun.

Not long before this I'd been to see him at Millfield. Academically it just wasn't working out for him – any more than it had for me – and he had his 'A' Levels coming up.

'Do you want to carry on?' I asked him.

'Not really, no,' he said and so he left. He started working even harder as an extra, as well as labouring and laying floors so he could pay to get his stunt register qualifications. I could have helped him out but I was so pleased to see his determination to do it all himself. Reminded me of someone else. I had wanted to see him get into special effects or camerawork – that seemed to be where the future was heading. I managed to get him an interview with Arthur Beavis – the special effects genius at Pinewood who I had met while working on *The Sweeney*. Arthur liked Franklin, and told him to go away and learn welding, and then come and see him once he'd finished school and he'd give him a start. Welding was considered an essential special effects skill back then because so many of the effects were physical rather than digital. I also got him an interview with Samuelson's Cameras – they were one of the top camera outfits for films and TV. Franklin didn't know anything about cameras, bless him, so I told him,

'Just go and pretend you know.' The interviewer said, kindly,

'We'll put you on the shortlist and call you in a couple of years.' That was in the 1980s and he's yet to hear back from them. Basically, he'd got the stunt bug, and he wanted to do what I was doing. He used to come and watch me turn cars over on shows like *The Sweeney* and *The Professionals*. It looked like fun to him and a good way to earn a living. He didn't take it too seriously to start with. That's probably why he's been so successful.

Back then there were far fewer people on the stunt register – about 70 or 80 – than the 500 on it today. Franklin had to qualify in six disciplines. The ones he chose were hang-gliding, horse riding, fencing, scuba, swimming and diving, and parachuting. Millfield had taught both fencing and horse riding, so he had a bit of a head start. Today you still need six disciplines but martial arts, including fighting up to brown belt standard, are compulsory.

Peter Brayham, his godfather, gave him his first job once he'd qualified – doubling Michael Caine on *Dr Jekyll and Mr Hyde*. Not a bad start. Franklin was already 6'1" and felt like he'd found his calling. As he put it to me recently,

'It's like playing cowboys and Indians and then you get paid. It's hard work with unsociable hours. You have good days and bad days; meet nice people and horrible people – just like any other job – but thankfully the nice outweigh the nasty by quite a way, which is why I've been doing it for nearly thirty years now.' Well said, son.

THE 1990s

The 1990s were a period of change for me. I wasn't getting any younger and the jobs weren't getting any easier. This didn't mean I slowed down. I worked throughout the decade on some tough jobs, but I could feel my body making louder protests with each passing year. I was so happy to see Franklin progress from job to job, really making his mark in the business. Right from the off he was good at stunt work. He picked things up so quickly – much faster than me – and got on with everyone he worked with. I was and am so proud of what he's achieved.

THE KRAYS (1990)

The decade started for me with a trip down memory lane. I'd got to know quite a lot of, shall we say, interesting people in the 60s, through some of the people I worked for in London in my youth. I'd done nothing violent, I hasten to add. So it was a bit like a case of *déjà vu*, working on this movie about the two most notorious criminals of their generation – Ronald and Reginald Kray, or Ronnie and Reggie, as they were widely known. The film was directed by Peter Medak, and Stuart St Paul was the stunt coordinator. I got on very well with both of them.

In one scene I was doubling for the brilliant actor Tom Bell who played Jack 'The Hat' McVitie, the twins' notorious henchman who they later murdered for messing up a job. In the scene he's driving away with his girlfriend, after getting a bollocking from the Krays. He ends up kicking his girlfriend out of the car for calling him 'bald'. Sy Hollands was the stuntwoman who played the girlfriend. My

God, she had some bottle – all she was wearing on her lower half was a miniskirt which offered little protection. We worked together a few times after that.

My second scene was more painful for me. It's McVitie's murder scene. He tries to escape by running into a window, but only gets so far as putting his head through the glass before he's dragged back into the room to be stabbed to death by Reggie. I had to do this a couple times to get it exactly how Peter wanted it. The first time I just went for it as usual – Lead Boot and all – and ended up going too far through the window. It was only supposed to be my head but I managed to get my shoulders through as well. Of course it was breakaway glass, which smashes easily, but you can still cut yourself on it if you're not careful. I felt bad because it took a while to reset everything but that's life on a movie set.

In another sequence where the Krays attack a rival gang with swords in a snooker hall, I got to work up close with the great Martin and Gary Kemp. Off-screen they were such friendly, lovely gents but as soon as the cameras rolled, they turned into their characters, just

Signed photo from the Kemp brothers, who I worked with on *The Krays*

like that. It was impressive. I even got to meet Charlie, the eldest of the Krays, briefly. As I said, I did get to know quite a lot of people in London. Years later, when a mutual friend of ours died, one of the hardest men in London attended his funeral. Sadly, he was on his last legs, too, in a wheelchair with an oxygen mask strapped to his face. God bless him for coming, though.

ROBIN HOOD: PRINCE OF THIEVES (1991)

This was my third Robin Hood. I also worked with Stevie Dent on the 2010 *Robin Hood*, starring Russell Crowe, and a much earlier TV version. Paul Weston, who was the stunt coordinator on *Prince of Thieves*, hired both me and my son – it was one of Franklin's first big stunt performances and certainly memorable for him, as I'll explain. One of the stunts I remember doing on *Prince of Thieves* was walking along and getting knocked over by Kevin Costner, the star of the film. He did it very well.

Franklin's experience was a bit different. It was his second proper job – he was a very new stuntman. The intake to the stunt register was about four that year, so they were regarded as cannon fodder by all and sundry.

Paul Weston needed someone to take a hit from Kevin Costner who, as Robin Hood, was escaping on a horse. That person was to be Franklin. As one of the Sheriff of Nottingham's men, he was posted on a castle gate. There's a fight and the sheriff's other men are shouting 'Close the gate!' to prevent Robin Hood getting away. So then Kevin Costner comes up on horseback, hits Franklin with a sack on his way out, and off he goes.

Then the Sheriff of Nottingham, played by the late and great Alan Rickman, comes and picks Franklin up, and starts beating him because he's so angry he let Robin Hood escape. It all went well in rehearsals but then they came to film it.

Kevin Costner comes galloping through, hits Franklin with the sack, he goes down. Fine. The Alan Rickman comes up, picks Franklin up and starts hitting him in the face – for real! Franklin's the new boy so he doesn't make a fuss.

So they shout, 'Cut!' and say *no, no, no, no – you can't do that.* They try to show Alan Rickman how to throw a punch. They go again. Kevin rides past, hits Franklin with the sack and he goes down. Again, the Sheriff of Nottingham comes up and...starts beating Franklin in the face!

'Cut!' The director, the actors, the other stunt performers are all surrounding poor Franklin, saying, *look, this is how you do it* to Alan Rickman. The director grabs Franklin by the shoulder and says to Alan,

'Watch this – this is how you throw a punch,' and now *he* lands one on Franklin. Everyone's on the floor laughing, including, I have to admit, me. So they just left it like that and moved on to the next sequence. The least you can say about that scene is that the punching looked real. Welcome to the register, Franklin!

KEEPING UP APPEARANCES (1990–1995)

When most people hear you're a stunt performer, they assume it's all hanging off helicopters and driving cars into ditches. Well, there is a lot of that, but there's also a lot of less spectacular action, which nevertheless needs to get done by someone other than the lead actors.

Keeping Up Appearances was a really well-made and much-loved British sitcom which ran for five series. It was a gentle comedy about a woman, Hyacinth Bucket (played by Patricia Routledge) who is desperate to climb the social ladder and impress people she considers to be upper-class. Unfortunately for her, her lower-class family keep holding her back. No wonder it was so popular in Britain, where everyone is obsessed with where you come from.

But it did really good business overseas as well. This is great for me, because I still to this day get repeat fees for programmes like this – so keep on *Keeping Up Appearances*, I say.

As I said, there is still a need for stunt performers on all sorts of programming, not just action films and thrillers. As a case in point, I remember a driving sequence in one of the episodes where Patricia/Hyacinth and her lower-class sister Daisy (Judy Cornwell) were sitting in the back, and I was doubling Daisy's husband, the lazy Onslow. There was also a special effects man in the car with a smoke gun. As we started filming there was a flash, so I pulled over and quickly got the actresses out of the car. Judy's hair was singed. Not too much harm done but they weren't keen to repeat the experience. Patricia's double asked if what we were doing was dangerous and I replied,

'Maybe a little.' It's a tough call in those situations because you don't want to let down the director or the stunt arranger, but you also don't want to mislead the other cast and crew, or else you end up losing their trust. And trust is paramount when you're asking actors to put themselves in your hands for the duration of a stunt – no matter how easy it may seem. Anyway, we reshot it with stunt doubles for the two ladies and it was fine.

The other thing I remember about this series was, like any series for the BBC, that it had a tight budget, so we had to scrimp and save wherever we could. We all had to get changed in front of each other – no trailers or star dressing rooms, as I recall. The cast and crew were all such lovely people and a tight-knit bunch. You often find that on TV series that have been going for a while. It becomes like another family. Ironically, in this one there was no snobbery at all.

VAN DER VALK (1992)

My part in this Dutch TV series was entirely unmemorable but it sticks in my mind because I'd put Franklin up for a job with Peter

Brayham. The stunt was eerily similar to the one which nearly ended my career prematurely in *Yellow Pages* (1984). Franklin was only 23 at the time.

It was a car stunt. Franklin had to drive up and off a ramp into the deep water of the Amsterdam docks. I recall that two American stuntmen had recently lost their lives doing something similar, so every precaution had been taken to ensure Franklin was safe. The Amsterdam fire brigade were on standby and there was a diver in the water.

Everyone was set, so Franklin revved the car up, drove very fast up onto the ramp and then down nose first into the harbour.

The windscreen burst under the pressure of water. This wasn't meant to happen. Peter Brayham – Franklin's godfather – watched in horror as his best friend's son slowly sank to the bottom of the docks – thirty feet of dark, cold murkiness. There was nothing he could do – he felt helpless as the seconds ticked by. The diver immediately slipped under to start searching for the car but visibility was appalling. To be honest, I don't think anyone had expected the car was going to sink.

Meanwhile, in the car, Franklin is showing composure way beyond his 23 years. He was scared but he knew he had to keep his head or he didn't have a chance. He had a diving cylinder tucked under his legs and he was trying to clear his ears as the car plummeted. When you're diving you wouldn't ideally wear a car as a weight belt and his ears were giving him a lot of pain, he said. He had the presence of mind to let the car settle. Thank God I'd told him to tie a small hammer to the dummy sitting next to him in the car. He smashed through the side window, took a couple of breaths from the cylinder, climbed through the broken window and kicked up for the surface. He knew the diver was looking for him, but he didn't want to wait around. He says that, when he surfaced, the first thing he saw was Brayham giving him the look of death – he had nearly died on his watch and Peter was furious. Franklin had been under for over five minutes. All I can say is they would have been the longest minutes of my life, so I can only imagine how bad Peter was feeling at the time. But I was so proud of how Franklin dealt with the situation. It shows how much he'd learned from us two old geezers.

BLUE ICE (1992)

I played a terrorist in this espionage thriller which starred the legendary Michael Caine. Franklin was doubling for the great man, as he had on his first job as an official stunt performer – the TV movie of *Jekyll and Hyde*.

He told me that he and Michael were in the make-up room one day and Caine turned to him and said, 'So you're my new stunt double?'

Franklin replied, 'Yes, but my dad doubled you years ago – on *The Black Windmill* (1974).' I'd had to double for Michael in a scene – running through a fire with a coat over my head.

Caine thought for a second, and then turned to the make-up ladies and said,

'Do you hear that? I'm working my way through the family!'

FILM v TV

I love working on both, but they are very different beasts. They're like two different circles which don't quite meet. Let's take money. On a film you get usually a one-off payment and you used to have to wait for years before it was shown again. That's changed of course, with DVDs and streaming.

Whereas you could be booked for a day on a TV series – say, The Bill, Coronation Street or EastEnders – and you will get a double fee because it's shown again on a Sunday, so you've doubled your money straightaway. You also might be finished by lunchtime whereas, on films, they tend to want their pound of flesh so you'll be there all day regardless, and it's a different atmosphere altogether. As someone said to me, TV is like, 'Would you mind? Could you?' whereas film is more like, 'We want you over there – NOW!' Yes, they're different animals altogether. Having said that, both have their good and bad points and I wouldn't have missed any experience I've had – except for the bad ones!

THE WORLD IS NOT ENOUGH (1999)

Franklin did some pretty hairy fire work on this, as I recall. I only had a couple of days' work, courtesy of Vic Armstrong, who was directing the second unit. Even so, my fourth James Bond – Pierce Brosnan – made quite an impression on me. The only scene we filmed together was him barging past me and knocking me down in the process. In real life, however, he was one of the nicest people I've ever met in the business. He went out of his way to introduce himself to people on set with him, and it was genuine – you can tell when someone's putting it on. He was a real gent and treated us all with respect, though not so much when he was in character!

THE 2000s

In the year 2000 I had my 64th birthday. I've continued to work to this day – both in and out of the movies, though I have finally slowed down a bit. Well, quite a lot, truth be told. My memory had given me problems since that dreadful accident in the 1980s. I still have some happy memories to share about the last couple of decades and – where I've forgotten some details – thankfully Franklin's usually been on hand to remind me, to fill in the gaps. This decade saw his life get ever busier as mine slowed down a bit. I'm so glad I was close by to see him at work in many of the great movies he coordinated on.

ROCKFACE (2002)

This TV drama about a mountain rescue team was Franklin's first stunt coordinator job. At this point he became a more senior figure in the business than me. He had our old friend Steve Dent to thank for it, but it's a mark of Franklin's ability that Steve trusted him this much.

They were standing chatting on a job one day and Steve's phone rang. He answered it and then said,

'Yeah, I've got the fella here for you.' It was a producer friend of Steve's – Kevan van Thompson – who was ringing to see if Steve could coordinate the TV show *Rockface*. Steve, who was greatly in demand as a coordinator, was already committed to another film but he said to Franklin,

'You use my equipment. That way, I get the hire and you get the job.' Franklin agreed. It became a great deal for a few years. Steve would get offered jobs he couldn't take on and he'd recommend Franklin who would take the job and then use Steve's gear so they split the deal. It was a great stepping stone for Franklin, too, as he got more important roles than he might have straightaway on his own, and this allowed him to build up a deservedly good reputation in the business.

Steve pulled a similar trick on Franklin when they were flying over to South Africa to work on a major studio picture a few years later. Once the plane had reached cruising altitude, Steve turned to Franklin and said,

'We won't be doing this film.'

'Oh, won't we?' said Franklin, looking puzzled.

'No, you will,' came the reply. I think Steve just liked to see the look on Franklin's face. 'I'll handle all the meetings and the budgeting and I'll leave you to do the coordination.'

'Oh, okay.'

So, they landed and met up with the team. This was a huge movie with a corresponding budget and a lot of stunt work to coordinate. Steve went to a production meeting telling Franklin,

'Right, standby.' In the meeting he told the director, 'I've got to go back to London but Franklin can take over for me.' The first assistant director had worked with Franklin on another major picture and vouched for him, and that was that. *Boom!* As they say, Franklin was coordinating his first major Hollywood picture. That's how this business works. You have to prove yourself and then you have to know the right people who can help you along. Then you become the one doing the helping.

SKY CAPTAIN (2004)

Franklin was the stunt arranger and I was his assistant. He was working with Jude Law and the main filming unit while I worked with the second unit.

I was there one day when Angelina Jolie came on set and walked up to Franklin and started chatting to him about a stunt they were working on like they were old mates. I had forgotten that they had hit it off on the *Tomb Raider* movies. It just showed me how far he'd come in a short period of time. He'd already gone way beyond my level of expertise and he was much more comfortable chatting to the actors than I had been at his age.

KING ARTHUR (2004)

I worked very hard for Steve Dent on this retelling of the Arthurian legend, which starred Clive Owen and Keira Knightley. Steve had given me quite a lot of riding scenes, and 14-hour days were the norm. Franklin was working on it, too. But my memories of the experience are clouded by what followed.

By the time I got back to West Sussex I was exhausted and looking forward to a couple of days to recuperate. It seems that life had other plans.

With the stunt team on *King Arthur*.
Was the smoky background trying to tell me something?

I'd gone for lunch and a chat with my old pal, Dickie Graydon. As I returned home I could see thick clouds of smoke coming from the village. As it was getting close to Halloween, I thought maybe someone had lit a bonfire prematurely, but deep down I think I knew that wasn't the case.

A policeman was stopping traffic on the edge of the village.

'Tell me it's not Dykes Farm,' I said to him.

'You'd better come with me, sir,' he said, ushering me through the checkpoint. A crowd of concerned villagers had gathered outside my drive. The house was badly damaged, with thick smoke billowing up from the buildings. Marion was shopping in London so I knew that she was safe. That was the main thing. I was also worried about my cat and my dogs but they were fine. Thankfully my neighbour Sue had phoned the fire brigade as soon as she saw what was happening. I did lose my aquarium with fourteen fishes in it, though, as well as many items of huge sentimental value including clocks that my grandfather had left me, photographs, books and furniture. I'd lost a book signed by Laurence Olivier and another one signed by John Wayne.

It turned out I had left a car battery on charge in my workshop and it had overcharged, exploding and setting fire to the lounge next door. We had a farm electricity supply and the cut-off switch had malfunctioned, causing the fire to start and then quickly get out of hand.

I must say the Hove Fire Service were brilliant. They were trialling a new foam that made extinguishing fire much faster, with less long-term damage. They battled the blaze for about four hours until it was under control.

It was a terrible shock – quite devastating at the time. The restoration cost me a five-figure sum, because I'd been in dispute with my insurance company about a claim and had refused to renew my home insurance policy as a result. Bad timing.

When I told Dickie what had happened he was as sympathetic as ever.

'That trip to visit you cost me fifty grand,' I said to him.

He chuckled and replied, 'Francis, if anyone can afford fifty big ones, it's you.'

The house was very badly damaged. However, Bruce Tighe, an old friend, helped me rebuild the house and did a terrific job – it was like my own personal Camelot by the time he'd finished. It still looks great to this day and – touch wood – we've had no incidents with fire since.

2 MB THE MIDDY October 30, 2003 www.midsussextoday.co.uk

£50,000 blaze caused by car battery

Stuntman owner's bid to enter burning home

A STUNTMAN to the stars had to be stopped from entering his house after his lounge burst into flames on Friday afternoon.

Frank Henson had just returned from filming a big budget Disney movie in Ireland when a car battery exploded in his workshop causing £50,000 of damage to his Poynings home.

Mr Henson had been charging the battery in his workshop when it exploded and destroyed the adjacent lounge at Dyke Farm.

Mr Henson said: "I didn't realise car batteries explode if you over-charge them. I hope other people can learn something from this."

Mr Henson had been driving home when he saw the smoke. He said: "I must have been at about Shaves Thatch when I saw the smoke. I thought someone had lit the village bonfire and was just praying it wasn't coming from Dyke Farm but soon realised it was."

Mr Henson rushed home and was relieved to find his dog and cats safe but was dismayed to learn his aquarium containing 14 goldfish had perished in the blaze. He also lost many items of sentimental value including photographs, paperwork and clocks left to him by his grandfather.

Frank, who has worked as a stuntman on many top Hollywood blockbusters including the James Bond films said he wanted to enter the building to recover some of his property. He said: "I got quite angry because they wouldn't let me in to the house. I wanted to get in to try and save some of my possessions. He added: "Both me and my son have got fire suits and I've been burned loads of times on my arms and my back and my son has suffered enormous burns while working."

Frank had returned from filming a new Disney film about King Arthur in Ireland. He said: "I'd had quite a hard week filming for about 14 hours a day and could have done without coming back to this. It's all been pretty grim really."

The fire service received numerous calls from members of the public and six appliances attended the scene at about 12.50pm. Keymer station commander Trevor Davey said: "The building was well alight and we concentrated our efforts to make sure it didn't spread to other parts of the house. The only task we could achieve when we got there was to save the house. In the end we were very, very pleased with what we would call a good stop."

Firefighters broke a hole in the roof of the house to release smoke, fumes and gases and Hove firefighters brought along a new type of foam which is on trial with the fire service which Mr Davey said "worked particularly well in fighting the fire."

The fire crews battled the blaze for about four hours until it was safe.

Work is already underway to repair the house.

FIRE SCENE: It was four hours before 'a good stop' was declared

Words by Patrick O'Donnell

Local paper report about the fire

THE CATHERINE TATE SHOW (2004)

This was a real tonic to the trauma of watching my house go up in flames. It may well be that the experience had aged me: I got the job because they were looking for an older stuntman, who looked like he might be dying. I thought, thanks very much. I'm so glad I took it on, though. Working with Catherine Tate was brilliant. I was playing a patient, Alfie, who was on his deathbed, unfortunately being attended to by her character, careless nurse Bernie. One of the scenes she had written in the script involved pushing me out of bed.

While we were rehearsing I said, 'Why don't you kick me out of bed?'

'Is that alright?' she asked.

'Yes, course it is!'

'Do you want any mats?'

'I'll be fine with my pads on.'

So she kicked me out of bed and we worked out how I could crawl back in without the cameras seeing me. I had some dialogue, too. Nurse Bernie tells me to go and clean out the toilets. I'd return breathing heavily, clasping the mop and bucket.

'I'm done now, can I get back into bed?'

Another patient in the ward sees what's going on and says,

'You can't make him do that, this man's dying!'

'That's alright,' she says, 'he's only cleaning the toilets.'

She was great at directing and working the scenes out, as well as being a brilliant comedian.

BASIC INSTINCT 2 (2006)

My son had been given the job on this film, mainly as a stuntman but after a week or so, the stunt coordinator badly hurt himself and Franklin took over. I did some car driving stunts for him. What I remember most about this film, though, was an incident involving another driver. It's a good example of why budgets for films can quickly escalate when something goes wrong.

Franklin was coordinating the opening sequence which involved a chase sequence with a Spyker C8 Laviolette kit car – a very expensive item. They go for over $200,000 I believe. The trouble is, the car had no traction. There's a long tunnel sequence where Sharon Stone's character is driving fast while getting it on with her near-comatose passenger. They wet the floors and then the stuntman doubling Sharon Stone – he was from the West Country – put his foot down and came hurtling around a corner in the Laviolette. He lost control, the car hit a bollard, spun around and then the back of the car hit the next bollard. Thankfully he wasn't badly hurt. He got out of the car, in a blonde wig, miniskirt up to here and said,

'I'm so sorry,' in a broad West Country accent. The car was a write-off but there was nothing he could have done. The cameraman whistled and observed,

'That's like smashing a Knightsbridge apartment into a wall.'

Franklin said,

'Thanks for that.'

THE COLOR OF MAGIC (2008)

Franklin had been offered the job as stunt coordinator on this Terry Pratchett fantasy adventure. He called me up and asked if I wanted to play a scene in which I was to be set on fire. It was going to be a bit like slapstick comedy. I agreed to do it just for the chance of meeting David Jason again – an actor I have so much respect for.

The job turned out a bit trickier than Franklin had let on.

The scenario was that there was a bar fight in this pub called The Broken Drum. During the fight the pub gets set on fire by a wizard or some such, and to illustrate this I have to rush out as the building burns and hop around behind David Jason while he chats away with another actor. Then I jump in a conveniently located water trough to extinguish the flames. This is all fine. I've done fire work before. It's dangerous and unpredictable but, as you've probably gathered by now, I'll do anything if I'm asked in the right way.

Anyway, what I didn't realise before accepting the part was that David Jason and the other actor were having a three-page conversation – not just an exchange about how hot it was getting out there! They had gelled me up and strapped me into the fireproof jacket. They say timing is everything and they were not wrong in this instance.

So David and his pal start chatting, the pub catches alight in the background, and then I emerge and hop around like a madman, flames wrapping around me while they carry on and finish this big dialogue scene, then I jump into the trough.

'Cut!' We had to do it a second time because I was screaming too loudly and the other actor couldn't hear David's dialogue properly. The second time we nailed it. By some miracle they hadn't messed up their lines and I had hit the cues exactly right.

The crew ran over and cooled down the fire-resistant clothes with a fire extinguisher before I could finally get out of them and dry off.

SHERLOCK HOLMES (2009)

Franklin was also stunt coordinator on this major movie update on the Sherlock Holmes character. Franklin had me doing a couple of days on set while he was working closely with director Guy Ritchie, mainly on the fight scenes in the film. They went through the script and broke the fights down by the different characters – opponents – that Sherlock Holmes, played in this movie by Robert Downey Junior, would be facing. Then Guy Ritchie said to Franklin,

'Give me three different fights – I want choices.' Franklin went away and worked out some different fight routines, and brought them back to Guy. He went through them and then for each fight sequence he said,

'I'll have this bit from that one, that bit from here, and this bit at the end of that fight. Put them all together and that's the fight I want for this sequence.'

'Excellent, we can do that,' said Franklin, and went away to organise it. It was like a pick'n'mix fight plan and it worked incredibly well, as you'll know if you've seen the film.

This film was a great example of how advances in technology have changed the stunt game.

The team were using these amazing high-speed, low-motion Phantom cameras which shot video at over 3,000 frames per second. I think they're even faster than that nowadays. When you slow it right down you still get brilliant detail – a single second can be stretched to up to fifty seconds – basically you see everything. All well and good. Except if you're trying to throw a stunt punch and get a reaction from the performer you're 'hitting'. There's no way it's going to work. It'll be obvious that you're faking it. This wouldn't have mattered if you were working with Alan Rickman (only joking) but otherwise it's going to give you a production headache.

Franklin was talking about it at the production meeting and in the end he said,

'Right, I'll get some stunt performers for you to look at to cast as McMurdo,' who Sherlock fights in the Punch Bowl scene. He had Dave Garrick and Brian Nickels lined up, but Guy Ritchie had his own ideas. He told Franklin,

'No, I want to use Joe Egan – Mike Tyson's old sparring partner.'

So, they started the rehearsals with Robert Downey Junior, who was playing Sherlock Holmes of course, and they got the fight all sorted out. *You go here and do this, then he'll come around here and do that*. It was all going well. Joe came in – a lovelier man you couldn't hope to meet – and they showed him the routine and he's getting it.

Then Robert Downey Junior came in and they hit it off and they're chatting away…and then they started the rehearsals. And Joe's forgotten the fight routine and is basically shaping up to Robert who's basically dodging all these punches which aren't meant to be coming his way, so they've stopped it.

And Franklin says,

'Um, I'm just going to go outside for a second.' As soon as he was outside he phoned the production office and said, 'Look, we can't use Joe. He's a lovely man but…' And the doors burst open and it's Robert and he says,

'I can't work with this guy,' and Franklin puts his hand over the phone and says, 'I know guvnor, I'm just sorting it out now,' and he said,

'Great.'

Anyway, they ended up getting Dave Garrick in – another ex-Para – who did a bit of sparring. When it came to the actual filming, Guy said,

'What are we going to do, then?' And Franklin replied,

'We're going to hit him – it's the only way. Dave knows and he's cool with it.' Robert Downey Junior said,

'I can't hit him. If you did that in America all the stunt guys would go mad.' But Franklin reassured him,

'No, no, no – it's alright.'

By the end of the fight scene, Dave's face was a bit puffy. Franklin went up to the producer who was really pleased with the scene. We stunt performers get 'adjustments' – or bonuses – for doing a nice job. Franklin said to him,

'Can I have an adjustment for Dave – can I give him 'x'? And the producer said,

'No. I think we should give him 'x+y',' and Franklin said,

'Thank you very much, sir.'

Dave was pleased, too.

CAROL WILKS

Carol Wilks is a fine director and producer who gave me a lot of work in British TV in the 2000s, including on hugely popular shows like The Bill, Heartbeat, Emmerdale and Coronation Street. She is one of my favourite people in the business, without a doubt. We always have a chat at Christmas time.

One of my memorable jobs for Carol was on Coronation Street, or Corrie as it's fondly called by fans of the show. I was playing Father Christmas, up on a roof, and I had to time my movement around a chimney stack just right, so I'd be seen by characters returning home after they'd had a long session in the pub. It was made trickier by the filming in the middle of the night, and it was also difficult for me to see them coming out of the pub from around the stack. Great fun, though.

In another episode I had to climb on a roof and I had a safety harness on which displeased the director, as it was in shot. So I took it off but then I slipped and slid down the roof until my legs were wrapped around the guttering. This was certainly a memorably painful experience, and looking back, I was probably quite lucky, though it didn't feel like it at the time. It also got me in trouble because I'd disobeyed the Health and Safety advisor!

I also recall being a drunk stuck in a tree who gets arrested by the police on The Bill, and tumbling over a cliff in the Yorkshire Dales with Steve Halliwell, the long-running Emmerdale cast member. Yes, having a head for heights was definitely an advantage when performing stunts for Carol, and she was always top of my list of people to work with.

HUGO (2011)

Martin Scorsese's historical adventure was a huge critical and commercial success. It was filmed in 3D which – like *Sherlock Holmes* – brought its own technical challenges and rewards. Martin Scorsese said in an interview somewhere the actors were very aware that every little move or gesture was picked up by the 3D cameras in a way that they wouldn't normally be.

I did about ten days' work on this and it was fascinating to watch the top stunt coordinators, Doug Coleman and Richard Bradshaw, at work. There were some very complicated stunts which weren't particularly dangerous but required an awful lot of planning and clever props. As I've said before, stunt work isn't always about the danger – in fact the whole point is to make something look good on-screen, which otherwise might be dangerous to perform, without compromising the health and safety of the actors.

I remember a scene on the railway platform where Sacha Baron Cohen, who was playing the dastardly station inspector, ended up putting his foot through about ten cellos before they got the scene exactly right. The cellos had a pre-drilled panel in them so his foot would go through easily. I'm guessing they weren't Stradivariuses!

VIKINGS (2016)

DETECTIVE PIKACHU (2019)

Even in my eighties I still like to get out and work. Thankfully there are still some people who need an old man with a lifetime's worth of experience to come and do the odd day's work. Franklin's been great to me. He always tries to fit me in if there's something suitable. I would never expect just to turn up, though. I always want to do a shift.

Franklin worked on *Vikings* for four and a half years. He had just finished *Gravity*, with Sandra Bullock and George Clooney, and went to make this little pilot for the show out in Ireland. He loved it and turned down some big films to stay on, because he was really enjoying the work and built up some fantastic relationships with the actors and crew. He got me over to do a few small parts. The most memorable was playing a fisherman on the edge of a settlement who is the first to be killed when the village is attacked by marauders. I had to take a couple of arrows to the chest.

Eventually he decided it was time to go back to feature films and he's been coordinating *Detective Pikachu*, a live-action Pokémon film starring Ryan Reynolds, which is set to be a big deal next year. I've done some falls on that – I can still get down with no problem but getting back up is more of a challenge.

With Franklin and the rest of the stunt crew on *Vikings*

MY FAVOURITE STUNTS

In over fifty years in the business I've seen and done everything. It's impossible to pick out a couple of stunts and say, 'These are the best ever.' Even so, there are some stunts which just stick with you. Not just for the level of spectacle – though that's important but for things like the artistry, the thinking behind the stunt or the courage it took to perform it. These are three of my favourites, in no particular order.

IIIIIIIIIIII

***PAUL WESTON – *crushed by a tank in* THE BEAST OF WAR (1988)** – *a film about a Soviet tank crew that get lost in an Afghanistan valley and then hunted down by Afghan rebels. I've written about this elsewhere (see page 142). The stunt is in a very tense scene where a rebel is executed by rolling a tank over him. Paul built a pit beneath the path of the tank and then judicious editing made it look as if the T-62 tank was slowly crushing him. It's a dangerous and visually stunning effect.*

IIIIIIIIIIII

***RICK SYLVESTER – *parachute jump in* THE SPY WHO LOVED ME (1977)** – *I've been in a few Bond films, so I know what's at stake, and how important the pre-title sequences are to the movie. I've done a bit of skiing and many parachute jumps, so I can also appreciate the technical difficulty of what he pulled off. Rick Sylvester was a mountaineer and not really a stunt performer at all, which makes his achievement even more remarkable.*

The sequence starts on top of a snow-covered mountain. Roger Moore's James Bond has just bid farewell to a warm cabin and hospitable young lady who, seconds later, radioes the villains to let them know he's on his way. He skis down a steep slope from the cabin until intercepted by the four gun-carrying skiers. Managing to dispatch a couple of them – with a bullet fired from a ski pole in one instance – Bond finds himself heading for a precipice. No problem. He jumps into the void, ditching his skis before opening a parachute on his back to display the Union Jack flag on the chute. One of the skis bounces off the chute just a second later. It could have gone horribly wrong on the one and only take, but thankfully it didn't. To manage to jump like that with the skis on – I thought he did brilliantly. Sylvester wasn't an experienced parachutist and he fell further than they had anticipated before pulling the cord. The main cameraman on a helicopter failed to get a shot of the chute opening, but thankfully a backup camera did. Epic stunt. And it was kind of replayed in the brilliant London Olympics opening ceremony, when 'The Queen' and 'James Bond' jump into the stadium from a helicopter with Union Jack parachutes. I should also mention the bungee jump off the Contra Dam in Switzerland, in GoldenEye (1995). A simple but stunning jump by stuntman Wayne Michaels.

IIIIIIIIIIII

***FRANKLIN HENSON – *wagon flip* in THE LEGEND OF ZORRO (2005) –** *This one took guts. The shot is this. A wagon pulled by two horses hurtles into shot. The driver is flung off the cartwheeling wagon in a trap set by Zorro. That's quite an ask and requires second-perfect timing. It's also not the kind of stunt you can properly rehearse – there are too many dynamic parts to it. A Canadian stunt performer had flipped the wagon and not quite got what the director – my old mate Martin Campbell – was after. The performer was also unfortunately injured in the process, taking a whack to the back of the head. He didn't want to make a second attempt. So Gary Powell, who was the stunt coordinator, got the stunt crew together and asked,*

'Who fancies a go?'

Franklin was the only person to step forward, which didn't surprise me. He's always been a bit fearless where stunts are concerned. A chip off the old block.

They were filming in Mexico where the weather is usually quite reliable. The first part of the scene, shot under a brilliant blue sky, was in the can. So what happened then? It got overcast. And stayed overcast. A week went by and then another one. There was a lot of standing around, sitting on the wagon when the skies brightened temporarily, staring at weather reports. The schedule was shifted around to fit in other bits of filming but all the while this major money shot was waiting to be completed. And with every day that went by, the cast and crew could feel the pressure increasing. When the skies cleared, they had to be ready to go, the horses had to be harnessed and the wagon axle wired up to the dead stop, and SFX cannon primed. In the end they had to wait three weeks for the weather to be right, so there was plenty of time for the nerves to build. Franklin also had his wife and three kids, who had travelled out with him at the start of the job, watching on set.

Finally the day came, though they couldn't be sure that clouds wouldn't reappear so everyone was a bit on edge. It was all marked out on the ground – where the wheels were going to be pulled out and where Franklin had to be off the wagon before the cannon fired to flip the wagon. He was sitting up in the seat, holding the reins. The cameras were so far away from the wagon they needed an intermediary. One of the stunt boys on horseback had the radio to let him know when the cameras were rolling and ready to go. They also had to be careful not to wind the horses up as they get to know the word 'action' and start to fidget. The outrider turned and shouted,

'That's us!' and he tore off.

Franklin gathered up the reins. He had two fiery ponies and had to keep them quiet and relaxed. The left-hand horse had other ideas. He reared up and lunged forward in the commotion – pulling the left rein out of his hand and took off at full speed. Franklin only had the right rein to steer with now. So he's going into the stunt action with only one rein and if he pulled on that one he was going down the ravine to the right of the set. He just had to go with it. The horses galloped on but not to the spot Gary had asked Franklin to get the wagon to before it was flipped. It got to the point of no return where he had to make a decision to go on or abandon. In that split second all sorts of possibilities go through your head. He stayed with it because, even though the stunt wasn't going to work properly, he could get at least get near where the sweet spot was. So, he jumped and was left lying there like an England footballer having just missed a crucial World Cup penalty. Gary Powell said,

'Don't worry, we'll do it again next week,' which made him feel a bit better.

The next time the weather cleared they were all set to go again. Franklin had got off the wagon and gone to move the mark for the wheels to come off further away, so the wheels would be ripped out underneath him as he jumped – rather than just before he jumped. He'd got himself really wound up by then. The walk back to the cart felt like the walk of a soccer player from the halfway line to take another decisive penalty. While he was doing that, Gary went and moved the marks back to their original positions, but Franklin didn't know this as his back was turned. John Wayne would not have approved but it worked.

'Rolling' and 'Action' were signalled over the radio and Franklin had time to get the reins gathered and the ponies under control and then geed them on, screaming at them to get them going faster.... Franklin smashed it. He hit the first mark – the wheels came off. The second mark he jumped up in the air, the cannon fired and the wagon flipped over right on cue. Everyone cheered under the piercing blue Mexican skies and they moved on to the next scene. One of the best stunts I've ever seen. It was a great moment for me. Gary did tell him he'd moved the marks after the job was done and they had a good laugh about it.

EPILOGUE

As I finish writing this book I'm living on the farm in Sussex that I bought many years ago. Looking out over the fields at the back of the house the land is mine as far as I can see.

Our house at Christmas – it's made a full recovery!

Serpico, my horse, is buried there. I've got four grandchildren – three boys and a girl and I love them all dearly. Callum – the eldest – is training to be a stunt performer. Clearly it's in the genes. I'm so proud. It makes me wonder what my father did – there were no stuntmen to speak of back then but I wonder if he did something similar?

It's a funny business. You're putting yourself at risk of injury and worse and yet you get very little recognition. You don't even get paid anywhere near as well as the people you're standing in for. So why do we do it? I'm no great thinker, but I guess there's something in most stunt performers which compels us to stand out from the crowd and prove ourselves, even if quite a few of the people I work with are really quite shy, like me. It's not that I wouldn't say boo to a goose but, as I've written elsewhere, the thought of standing in front of a camera and reciting lines terrifies me much more than falling off a bridge or turning a car over.

I think by and large we're happy for others to get the public recognition. It would probably spoil the movie magic if the audiences knew just how often the person they see on-screen is the stunt pro or double, rather than the world-famous Hollywood actor. One thing I think is true is that we stunt crews crave the recognition of our fellow performers and love the camaraderie of a stunt crew on location. After all, you see the same faces year after year and we all get to know each other's strengths and weaknesses.

You meet the odd bad apple but I can honestly say they are few and far between. The stunt performers I've worked with over the years – the ones mentioned in this book and others almost too numerous to mention – have been the best working buddies you could hope for. There's competition for jobs and jockeying for position like in any line of work, but there's just as much watching each other's backs and looking out for each other, too. At the end of the day, you're relying on someone else for your safety and next time it will probably be them that's relying on you. So you do your best at all times.

The industries changed a lot since I started out. In the early days it was mainly ex-military types who did the stunt work. Safety was in the hands of the director. Now it's a proper industry with training skills required and a register of all those performers allowed to work on film and TV productions. Even when you've qualified to be on the register you're still on probation for three years, required to work under the supervision of a stunt coordinator. I think this is a good thing and as a result there are very few fatal accidents these days. Cuts and bruises? That's another story. They're par for the course, same as getting knife cuts or burns as a chef.

Tragedies do happen, nevertheless. A close pal of mine – Tip Tipping – was killed working on the BBC's *999* programme. The terrible irony is he was re-creating a parachute accident that went wrong when he fell to his death. That hit me badly.

With Tip Tipping, a great friend and much missed

I've lost other colleagues to accidents and even suicide. That's the darker side of the business: it can attract people who use the adrenalin surges as an escape from issues which plague them, like depression. Hopefully, as we come to understand these conditions more deeply, such situations will be managed better. But it's a great life and I'd recommend it to anyone who's prepared to put in the training and the hard work to make it onto the register and beyond. No one day is like another. You learn new skills all the time as the equipment and technology develop. It really is like no other business.

Nowadays I like to keep myself busy working on the farm. I wake up in the morning at 8am and head over there to do some mucking out or other small tasks. I like to keep fit and healthy and so, although the bones make creak a bit, I can still do the odd day's stunt work. I have never smoked in my life and I rarely drink, though I do like a drop of Guinness on a Sunday afternoon with good friends, especially when the conversations are flowing. I don't condemn anyone that does drink and smoke as everyone has their own lifestyle.

I still own some properties in London and have an apartment in Spain, not far from Barcelona, that myself and my wife visit a couple of times a year. We love it out there.

Travel's been a really important part of my life. When you go to other countries and see how other people live it gives you a better understanding of the world and also of the country you live in. That's why, even though I was in the Paras, meeting American military veterans and seeing how they were treated made me very anti-war.

If I could pass on one message to anyone reading this it would probably be never underestimate yourself, or other people. I came from the poorest of backgrounds with none of the advantages we take for granted these days. We're all different but also – deep down – not much different from each other.

If you've got the drive and determination you can make your dreams come true – just don't let anything get in your way. If you fall at the first hurdle, pick yourself up and start again. Believe me, you'll get there in the end. And treat people well. Don't think you're better than someone else because of where they come from or how they speak. If you're open to them then they will be more open to you.

Being on a film set has taught me that. Some of the biggest stars I've worked with – John Wayne, Pierce Brosnan, Carrie Fisher, Harrison Ford, Lewis Collins – never looked down on the crew or took advantage of their star status. Quite the opposite. They mucked in and worked hard to make the best film possible. As a result they earned the respect of everyone they worked with. That's got to be a much better feeling than being stuck in your trailer and only coming out when you're called. It's a great approach for anyone in life.

I've come a long way from that Whitehawk estate, even if it's just a few miles down the road from the farm. It's been a great journey and I hope you've enjoyed reading about it. Now, if you'll excuse me, I've got some horses to muck out.

Me and Marion with a fan at a Star Wars Fan Fun Day

Frank Henson, October 2018

APPENDIX

– FILM, ACTING AND TV CREDITS

This is a list of the films and TV programmes I've worked on, either as a stunt performer or, in some rare instances, as an actor. It's not comprehensive, so apologies if you're sitting watching a rerun of an old Seventies crime thriller and you think to yourself, 'Isn't that Frank Henson?' My memory's not what it was and so I've probably missed a few, but I think all the important ones are here!

THE GUNS OF NAVARONE (1961)
Director: J. Lee Thompson
Stunt performer (Stunt coordinator: Joe Powell)

YOU ONLY LIVE TWICE (1967)
Director: Lewis Gilbert
Stunts (uncredited)

ROBBERY (1967)
Director: Peter Yates
Stunts (uncredited)

CARRY ON FOLLOW THAT CAMEL (1967)
Director: Gerald Thomas

WHERE EAGLES DARE (1968)
Director: Brian G. Hutton
Stunts (uncredited)
Acting credit: Legionnaire

Z CARS (1968) (TV series)
Acting credit: Trevor Robins

MONTE CARLO OR BUST
(Those Daring Young Men in Their Jaunty Jalopies) (1969)
Director: Ken Annakin
Stunt performer

CATWEAZLE (1970) (TV series)
Acting credit: Norman soldier

STRAW DOGS (1971)
Director: Sam Peckinpah
Stunt performer (Stunt coordinator: Bill Cornelius)

THE BLACK WINDMILL (1974)
Director: Don Siegel
Acting credit: S. P. Driver

ONE OF OUR DINOSAURS IS MISSING (1975)
Director: Robert Stevenson
Stunt performer

BRANNIGAN (1975)
Director: Douglas Hickox
Stunt performer and stunt driver

THE SWEENEY (1975-1978) (TV series)
(Stunt arranger: Peter Brayham)
Stunt performer, stunt driver, vehicle stunt coordinator

SPACE: 1999 (1975-1977) (TV series)
Stunt performer (Stunt coordinator: Peter Brayham)
Acting credit: Security guard

AT THE EARTH'S CORE (1976)
Director: Kevin Connor
Stunt performer

SKY RIDERS (1976)
Director: Douglas Hickox
Stunt performer (Stunt coordinator: Peter Brayham)

STAR WARS EPISODE IV – A NEW HOPE (1977)
Director: George Lucas
Stunt performer (Stunt coordinator: Peter Diamond)
Acting credit: Storm trooper, Biker Scout

TARGET (1977) (TV SERIES)
Acting credit: Eddy

BLAKE'S 7 (1978) (TV series)
Stunt performer

LAW & ORDER (1978) (TV miniseries)
Acting credit: Frank Ryan/Security Guard

THE PROFESSIONALS (1978-83) (TV series)
Stunt arranger and performer (Stunt arranger: Peter Brayham)

QUADROPHENIA (1979)
Director: Franc Roddam
Stunt performer
Acting credit: Postman

DRACULA (1979)
Director: John Badham
Stunt performer
Acting credit: Sailor (on The Demeter)

THE DICK FRANCIS THRILLER: THE RACING GAME (1979) (TV series)
Acting credit: Third Heavy

THE LONG GOOD FRIDAY (1980)
Director: John Mackenzie
Stunt performer (Stunt coordinator: Roy Alon)

SHOESTRING (1979-80) (TV series)
Stunt performer and arranger

JULIET BRAVO (1980-83) (TV series)
Stunt performer
Acting credit: Villain

AN AMERICAN WEREWOLF IN LONDON (1981)
Director: John Landis
Stunt performer (Stunt coordinator: Vic Armstrong)

GREAT EXPECTATIONS (1981)
Director: Julian Amyes
Stunt performer (Stunt arranger: Peter Brayham)

TALES OF THE UNEXPECTED (1980) (TV series)
Stunt coordinator and performer
Acting credit: Van driver

SAFARI 3000 (1982)
Acting credit: English Team (Stunt coordinator: Peter Brayham)

STAR WARS – RETURN OF THE JEDI (1982)
Director: George Lucas
Stunt performer (Stunt coordinators: Peter Diamond & Glen Randall Jr)

GRANGE HILL (1983) (TV series)
Fight arranger (Episode 6.1, Director: Carol Wilks)

OCTOPUSSY (1983)
Director: John Glen
Stunt performer

NEVER SAY NEVER AGAIN (1983)
Director: Irvin Kershner
Stunt performer (Stunt coordinator: Vic Armstrong)

INDIANA JONES AND THE TEMPLE OF DOOM (1984)
Director: Steven Spielberg
Stunt performer (Stunt arrangers: Vic Armstrong & Glen Randall)

TOP SECRET (1984)
Directors: Jim Abrahams, David Zucker, Jerry Zucker
Stunt performer (Stunt coordinator: Joe Powell)

THE AMBASSADOR (1984)
Director: J. Lee Thompson
Stunt arranger and performer (Stunt coordinator: Peter Diamond)

GOING UNDERCOVER
(originally known as YELLOW PAGES) (1985)
Director: James Kenelm Clarke
Stunt performer (Stunt coordinator: Jim Dowdall)

KING SOLOMON'S MINES (1985)
Director: J Lee Thompson
Stunt performer (Stunt coordinator: Peter Diamond)

MR. LOVE (1985)
Director: Roy Battersby
Stunt coordinator

BRAZIL (1985)
Director: Terry Gilliam
Stunt performer (Stunt arranger: Bill Weston)

SUPERGRAN (1985) (TV series)
Stunt performer (13 episodes)

A VIEW TO A KILL (1985)
Director: John Glen
Stunt performer (Stunt team supervisor: Bob Simmons)

WILD GEESE II (1985)
Director: Peter Hunt
Stunt performer (Stunt arranger: Dickey Beer)

LIFEFORCE (1985)
Director: Tobe Hooper
Stunt performer (Stunt arranger: Peter Diamond)

REVOLUTION (1985)
Director: Hugh Hudson
Stunt performer

EDGE OF DARKNESS (1985)
Director: Martin Campbell
Stunt performer

ENEMY MINE (1985)
Director: Wolfgang Petersen
Acting credit: Lump
Stunt performer

WHOOPS APOCALYPSE (1986)
Director: Tom Bussmann
Stunt performer (Stunt coordinator: Gareth Milne)

RAWHEAD REX (1986)
Director: George Pavlou
Stunt performer (Stunt coordinator: Peter Brayham)

CASUALTY (1986)
Stunt performer and arranger

THE LIFE AND LOVES OF A SHE-DEVIL (1986) (TV series)
Director: Philip Saville
Stunt arranger and performer

HALF MOON STREET (1986)
Director: Bob Swaim
Stunt performer
Acting credit: SAS Man

THE LIVING DAYLIGHTS (1987)
Director: John Glen
Stunt performer (Stunt supervisor: Paul Weston)

LIONHEART (1987)
Director: Franklin J. Schaffner
Stunt performer (Stunt coordinator: Peter Diamond)

THE MARKSMAN (1987) (TV series)
Director: Tom Clegg
Stunt performer

FULL METAL JACKET (1987)
Director: Stanley Kubrick
Stunt performer

AMSTERDAMNED (1988)
Director: Dick Maas
Stunt performer (Stunt coordinator: Dickey Beer)

WILLOW (1988)
Director: Ron Howard
Stunt performer (Stunt coordinator: Gerry Crampton)

WHO FRAMED ROGER RABBIT (1988)
Director: Robert Zemeckis
Stunt performer (Stunt arranger: Peter Diamond)

THE BEAST OF WAR (1988)
Director: Kevin Reynolds
Stunt performer (Stunt coordinator: Paul Weston)

WITHOUT A CLUE (1988)
Director: Thom Eberhardt
Stunt performer (Stunt coordinator: Paul Weston)

STAR TRAP (1988) (TV movie)
Director: Tony Bicât
Stunt performer
Acting credit: Evil man

BERGERAC (1989) (TV series)
Stunt performer

NIGHTBREED (1990)
Director: Clive Barker
Stunt performer

THE KRAYS (1990)
Director: Peter Medak
Stunt performer (Stunt coordinator: Stuart St Paul)

ROBIN HOOD: PRINCE OF THIEVES (1991)
Director: Kevin Reynolds
Stunt performer (Stunt coordinator: Paul Weston)

KEEPING UP APPEARANCES (1991) (TV series)
Stunt performer

THE BILL (1991)
Acting credit: Martin

VAN DER VALK (1991-2) (TV series)
Stunt performer (2 episodes) (Dangerous Game, Director: Jim Goddard; Poor of Life, Director: Tom Clegg; stunt arranger: Peter Brayham)

SHADOWCHASER (1992)
Director: John Eyres
Stunt performer (Stunt coordinator: Terence Plummer)

BOON (1991–2) (TV series)
Stunt performer (Stunt arranger: Paul Weston)

BETWEEN THE LINES (1992) (TV series)
Director: Alan Dosser
Stunt performer (Stunt arranger: Tip Tipping)

BLUE ICE (1992)
Director: Russell Mulcahy
Acting credit: Terrorist

THE BRITTAS EMPIRE (1993) (TV series)
Director: Mike Stephens
Stunt performer

SHUTTLECOCK (1993)
Director: Andrew Piddington
Stunt performer

THE HAWK (1993)
Director: David Hayman
Stunt performer (Stunt coordinator: Peter Brayham)

TIME AFTER TIME (1994) (TV series)
Stunt performer

SHOPPING (1994)
Director: Paul Anderson
Stunt performer (Stunt coordinator: Jim Dowdall)

DEATH MACHINE (1994)
Director: Stephen Norrington
Stunt performer (Stunt coordinator: Stuart St Paul)

THIEF TAKERS (1995) (TV series)
Stunt performer

ELIDOR (1995) (TV series)
Stunt arranger (Co-stunt arranger: Andy Bradford)

THE TOMORROW PEOPLE (1995) (TV series)
Director: Crispin Reece
Stunt double

PIE IN THE SKY (1995) (TV series)
Stunt performer (Stunt coordinator: Peter Diamond)

FIST OF FUN 1995 (TV series)
Stunt performer

DANGERFIELD (1996) (TV series)
Director: Jim Goddard
Stunt performer & stunt coordinator ('Tricks')
(Stunt coordinator: Peter Diamond)

GADGETMAN (1996) (TV movie)
Director: Jim Goddard
Stunt coordinator

THE BORROWERS (1997)
Director: Peter Hewitt
Stunt performer (Stunt coordinator: Jim Dowdall)

SPICE WORLD (1997)
Director: Bob Spiers
Stunt performer (Stunt coordinator: Peter Brayham)

HEARTBEAT (1998) (TV series)
Stunt coordinator; fight arranger & coordinator

GET REAL (1998)
Director: Simon Shore
Stunt coordinator

BARBARA (1999) (TV series)
Director: Richard Boden
Stunt performer
Acting credit: Builder

THE WORLD IS NOT ENOUGH (1999)
Director: Michael Apted
Stunt performer (Stunt coordinator: Vic Armstrong)

A MANY SPLINTERED THING (2000) (TV series)
Stunt coordinator (2 episodes)

THE STRETCH (2000)
Director: Frank W. Smith
Stunt performer (Stunt coordinator: Peter Diamond)

DOWN TO EARTH (2001) (TV series)
Acting credit: Dave Hartford

MIDSOMER MURDERS (2003) (TV series)
Director: Sarah Hellings
Stunt performer (Painted in Blood) (Stunt coordinator: Colin Skeaping)

SKY CAPTAIN AND THE WORLD OF TOMORROW (2004)
Director: Kerry Conran
Co-stunt coordinator with Franklin Henson

THE CATHERINE TATE SHOW (2004)
Stunt performer

DOT.KILL (2005)
Director: John Irvin
Stunt performer

BASIC INSTINCT 2 (2006)
Director: Michael Caton-Jones
Stunt performer (Stunt coordinators: Andy Bradford, Franklin Henson)

CHILDREN OF MEN (2006)
Director: Alfonso Cuarón
Stunt performer

BREAKING AND ENTERING (2006)
Director: Anthony Minghella
Stunt performer (Stunt coordinator: Steve Dent)

FLYBOYS (2006)
Director: Tony Bill
Stunt performer (Stunt coordinator: Franklin Henson)

HOLBY CITY (2006) (TV series)
Stunt coordinator

THE GOLDEN COMPASS (2007)
Director: Chris Weitz
Stunt performer (Stunt coordinators 2nd unit: Vic Armstrong, Wendy Armstrong)

NATIONAL TREASURE: BOOK OF SECRETS (2007)
Director: Jon Turteltaub
Stunt performer (Stunt coordinator: George Ruge)

THE COLOR OF MAGIC (2008)
Stunt performer (Stunt coordinator: Franklin Henson)

FOUR SEASONS (2008) (TV miniseries)
Director: Giles Foster
Stunt coordinator

SHERLOCK HOLMES (2009)
Director: Guy Ritchie
Stunt performer (Stunt coordinator: Franklin Henson)

---

10 MINUTE TALES (2009) (TV series)
Stunt coordinator

THE WOLFMAN (2010)
Director: Joe Johnston
Stunt performer (Stunt coordinators: Wendy Armstrong, Steve Dent)

ROBIN HOOD (2010)
Director: Ridley Scott
Stunt performer (Stunt coordinator: Rob Inch)

THE BILL (2010)
Stunt coordinator (2 episodes)

NEVER LET ME GO (2010)
Director: Mark Romanek
Stunt coordinator

ONE DAY (2011)
Director: Lone Scherfig
Stunt performer (Stunt coordinator: Jim Dowdall)

SHERLOCK HOLMES: A GAME OF SHADOWS (2011)
Director: Guy Ritchie
Stunt performer (Stunt coordinator: Franklin Henson)

HUGO (2011)

Director: Martin Scorsese

Stunt performer (Stunt coordinator: Doug Coleman)

THE FILM-MAKER'S SON (2013)

Director: Bart Gavigan

Acting credit: Watchman

CATHERINE TATE'S NAN (2014)

Acting credit: Alfie

PENNY DREADFUL (2014-2016) (TV series)

Stunt performer (Stunt coordinator: Peter Miles)

VIKINGS (2013-2016) (TV series)

Stunt performer ('Trial' (2013)); 'The Uncertain Hour Before Morning' (2016) (Stunt coordinator: Franklin Henson)

IMAGE PERMISSIONS

Where a photographic credit is required, and I've known the source, I've included it. A lot of effort has been made to track down the ownership of the photographs but some have got lost in the mists of time. If you're the photographer for any of these images, and you haven't been credited, please let me know and I'll make sure there's a proper credit in the next run of the book.

In the *Return of the Jedi* section [pp90–106], photos labelled COURTESY OF LUCASFILM LTD.LLC are used with permission and under the Copyright and Trademark Notice: *Star Wars: Episode VI – Return of the Jedi ã* &ä 1983 and 1997 Lucasfilm Ltd. LLC.

ACKNOWLEDGEMENTS

I hope you've enjoyed reading this as much as I've enjoyed writing it.

I have wanted to put my thoughts and memories on paper for a long time. As I've said elsewhere, if I could pass on one message to you, the reader, no matter what age or background you're from, it's that hard work is the easiest route to achieving what you want in life. If you persevere you'll get there in the end.

The journey that this book went on is a good example of that, in practice. I had a couple of false starts but I didn't get disheartened, even though it seemed to be going nowhere for a while. Then a young friend, Stephen Phillips, helped me get many of my thoughts down on paper. I now had enough to take to a publisher – SPP in Bath. They put me in touch with Simon Toseland – an award-winning ghostwriter – who has helped me along the rest of the way to the book you see before you now.

I'd like to thank everyone who has been involved in the book – particularly Simon and Stephen – and also the many friends and colleagues who have responded to Simon's questions about films we worked on together. This includes Vic Armstrong, Paul Weston, Jim Dowdall, Tracey Eddon and, of course, my son Franklin. I'd also like to thank all the people who have written to me over the years, with questions about films I've worked on and messages telling me how much they've enjoyed them. It really means a lot.

I've included a lot of photos from my private collection – they may not all be great quality, but they give a flavour of the times. Sadly, there are a lot of films for which I don't have any photographic record. Taking pictures wasn't always as easy as it is today, of course, and you didn't always think to pack a camera wherever you went.

Thankfully I've got some nice pictures from *Return of the Jedi* – that's because I was determined to enjoy my first trip to the States. I also have Vic Armstrong to thank for allowing me to use some of his pictures taken on the set of *Indiana Jones and the Temple of Doom*. I lost quite a lot of photos in the fire we had here at the farm.

Finally, I'd like to acknowledge the love and support of my family and in particular my dear wife, Marion, without whom I wouldn't have achieved much in my life – she has been my friend and inspiration since we were married over 50 years ago.

Frank Henson
October 2018